The United States Army War College

The United States Army War College educates and develops leaders for service at the strategic level while advancing knowledge in the global application of Landpower.

The purpose of the United States Army War College is to produce graduates who are skilled critical thinkers and complex problem solvers. Concurrently, it is our duty to the U.S. Army to also act as a "think factory" for commanders and civilian leaders at the strategic level worldwide and routinely engage in discourse and debate concerning the role of ground forces in achieving national security objectives.

The Strategic Studies Institute publishes national security and strategic research and analysis to influence policy debate and bridge the gap between military and academia.

The Center for Strategic Leadership contributes to the education of world class senior leaders, develops expert knowledge, and provides solutions to strategic Army issues affecting the national security community.

The Peacekeeping and Stability Operations Institute provides subject matter expertise, technical review, and writing expertise to agencies that develop stability operations concepts and doctrines.

The School of Strategic Landpower develops strategic leaders by providing a strong foundation of wisdom grounded in mastery of the profession of arms, and by serving as a crucible for educating future leaders in the analysis, evaluation, and refinement of professional expertise in war, strategy, operations, national security, resource management, and responsible command.

The U.S. Army Heritage and Education Center acquires, conserves, and exhibits historical materials for use to support the U.S. Army, educate an international audience, and honor Soldiers—past and present.

STRATEGIC STUDIES INSTITUTE

The Strategic Studies Institute (SSI) is part of the U.S. Army War College and is the strategic-level study agent for issues related to national security and military strategy with emphasis on geostrategic analysis.

The mission of SSI is to use independent analysis to conduct strategic studies that develop policy recommendations on:

- Strategy, planning, and policy for joint and combined employment of military forces;

- Regional strategic appraisals;

- The nature of land warfare;

- Matters affecting the Army's future;

- The concepts, philosophy, and theory of strategy; and,

- Other issues of importance to the leadership of the Army.

Studies produced by civilian and military analysts concern topics having strategic implications for the Army, the Department of Defense, and the larger national security community.

In addition to its studies, SSI publishes special reports on topics of special or immediate interest. These include edited proceedings of conferences and topically oriented roundtables, expanded trip reports, and quick-reaction responses to senior Army leaders.

The Institute provides a valuable analytical capability within the Army to address strategic and other issues in support of Army participation in national security policy formulation.

Strategic Studies Institute
and
U.S. Army War College Press

U.S. LANDPOWER IN THE SOUTH CHINA SEA

Clarence J. Bouchat

July 2017

*****

This manuscript was funded by the U.S. Army War College External Research Associates Program.

ISBN 978-1977877895

FOREWORD

In his third Strategic Studies Institute (SSI) monograph addressing turmoil in the South China Sea region, retired U.S. Air Force officer Clarence J. Bouchat counters the misperceptions that U.S. landpower plays only a minor or supporting role in what is normally considered a predominately maritime- and air-centric theater. Conventional wisdom's misunderstanding of how modern and future landpower capabilities may influence engagement and operations in semi-enclosed maritime environments may be the cause for landpower being marginalized in these environments, as seen in the original Air-Sea Battle concept or the 2014 *Quadrennial Defense Review* (QDR).

For that reason, I am pleased to present this monograph, which explains the vital role of landpower to engage the forces of other countries, deter aggression, and fight if necessary in pursuit of broad U.S. national interests in the region. In a variety of ways described here, the essential direct support of land force capability to the air and sea services, and other government organizations, is also critical to their success when operating in this theater. As Mr. Bouchat states in his Introduction, landpower "offers important options which can often be applied with lower risk of exacerbating direct conflict. As the only form of military power that covers the full range of military options, from humanitarian assistance to full conventional combat, landpower's flexibility and capabilities help manage both peace and conflict" in the South China Sea.

To show how landpower is necessary in this contested region, this monograph briefly explores the concept of landpower and its components—forces from the U.S. Army, U.S. Marine Corps, and U.S. Special Operations Command (USSOCOM). It then examines landpower's contributions to potential combat operations through wide area defense and maneuver to deterrence through forward presence and peacetime operations, and security engagement with the region's landpower-dominant allies, partners, and competitors. With this understanding of landpower's capabilities to support national interests in a semi-enclosed maritime environment and recommendations to improve its potential in air-sea environments, the reader will better understand that landpower's supporting and stabilizing role is especially important in a theater like the South China Sea.

DOUGLAS C. LOVELACE, JR.
Director
Strategic Studies Institute and
    U.S. Army War College Press

ABOUT THE AUTHOR

CLARENCE J. BOUCHAT is a retired U.S. Air Force officer, and an adjunct instructor at the U.S. Army War College (USAWC) Department of Distance Education. He served in several assignments in East Asia, including the American Embassy in Kuala Lumpur. He has taught strategy, geography, and East Asia studies at the University of Maryland University College, Harrisburg Area Community College, and his alma mater the U.S. Air Force Academy. He is the author of several works on the South China Sea, and developer of the political-military board game *South China Sea* in support of a course he teaches on this region. He is also a Wiki Supervisor and senior analyst for the crowd-sourced strategic intelligence consultancy Wikistrat Inc.

SUMMARY

U.S. landpower in the South China Sea is an essential component to stabilizing this contested region. Together, the U.S. Army, Marine Corps, and Special Operations Forces (SOF) offer distinctive capabilities whose defensive nature in this semi-enclosed maritime environment tend to be less prone to escalation while still sending an unequivocal message of committed support and steady resolve to partners and competitors alike. To establish U.S. landpower as a critical part of security and stability in the region, this monograph presents how its wide-ranging capabilities are important in directly supporting U.S. interests. Even in a sea- and air-dominated environment, landpower's broad operational and diverse support capabilities in pursuit of increasingly interdependent joint and unified operations make it an indispensable element in attaining U.S. interests. Landpower may be the most decisive, flexible, and versatile force through full spectrum operations, fully covering the range from humanitarian assistance to conventional state-on-state warfare; landpower is also crucial to understanding, engaging, and influencing people and leaders. U.S. landpower holds special influence because land forces dominate this region's military structure.

The first of the strategic roles of landpower, to compel or fight and win decisively, is more important than is normally credited in a maritime environment. The U.S. Army provides indispensable support to other forces and agencies through its theater opening and sustaining abilities. Through its core competency of wide area security, U.S. landpower is responsible for passive and active means to protect against external and internal threats. The Army's air and missile defense systems are particularly needed in this anti-access area-denial (A2AD) environment against pre-emptive strikes. The security role of sea control from the land through anti-ship missiles is a historic and influential one in a semi-enclosed sea environment, but still needs to be operationally developed by U.S. land forces. The counterland mission through surface-to-surface missiles acts as a shield to suppress close-in attack systems located around the region. Another core competency is combined arms maneuver. Amphibious operations are a useful option during disasters and in the periphery of combat operations around the South China Sea. Maneuver by air offers another option, but is also vulnerable in the current threat environment. Landpower's combat capability is a measure of last resort, but does give credibility to landpower's deter and engage strategic roles.

The second of the strategic roles of U.S. landpower, to deter and prevent war, is also crucial to stability in Southeast Asia. Deterrence needs to exhibit the will to back combat capabilities, which is demonstrated through the forward presence of troops and prepositioning of equipment and supplies. The advantages of forward positioning can be gained through using hardened, dispersed, or temporary facilities. U.S. landpower's ability to help mitigate crises and contingencies, whether security related or from natural or manmade disasters, is another means to show its resolve and capability in the region. The importance of landpower to deterrence and preventing war is due to the resolve that land forces represent when committed by the U.S. Government. With forward presence and the operational interaction with the forces of Southeast Asia, U.S. forces have more opportunity to assure partners.

U.S. landpower's strategic role to engage states and shape conditions may well reduce the need for deterrence or combat. Through security cooperation and engagement activities, regional states may better understand each other and ensure stability and security to address U.S. and regional states' interests. U.S. landpower builds partner capacity through interpersonal and organizational engagements. Security cooperation activities also help to develop the capabilities of friendly forces and regional interoperability through security assistance from the United States. The forward presence of U.S. land forces reinforces the strengths and advantages of shaping and engagement activities. Although all three U.S. landpower strategic roles—combat and compel, deter and prevent, and engage and shape—are mutually dependent upon each other, engage and shape may be the most important in stabilizing the disputes in the South China Sea.

The use of landpower to address the disputes in the South China Sea is not usually considered in what is typically labeled a maritime- and air-centric theater, but the role of U.S. landpower is profound in this arena, and its influence will be undeniable in preventing war; or, should that fail, winning the peace.

U.S. LANDPOWER IN THE SOUTH CHINA SEA

"Speak softly but carry a big stick."
—Theodore Roosevelt, U.S. President, 1901.

INTRODUCTION[1]

The use of landpower to help shape the disputes in the South China Sea is not usually considered in what is typically labeled a maritime- and air-centric theater. The conventional wisdom of media, political, academic, and even military participants in the South China Sea debate is headlined by the U.S. military concept of Air-Sea Battle that was developed to ensure freedom of access to the region.[2] In part, this wisdom is based on the fact that within the 122,648,000 nautical square miles encompassing the South China Sea, there are less than 5 square miles of naturally occurring land in the Spratly and Paracel Islands, with China's current controversial contributions nearly doubling that land mass but only adding a tiny fraction overall.[3] To further emphasize the point, no U.S. Army or Marine Corps general officer has ever commanded U.S. Pacific Command (USPACOM), and the U.S. Army only recently upgraded its senior officer in the Pacific region to the rank of full General in 2013.[4] Even the Department of Defense's (DoD) foundational 2014 *Quadrennial Defense Review* (QDR) report only mentions landpower in East Asia in terms of its well-established presence in Northeast Asia.[5] Between vast ocean distances and institutional neglect, what is the role of ground forces in the South China Sea compared to the seemingly better-suited platforms of air and naval forces?

U.S. landpower in the South China Sea should not be overlooked, because it offers important options that can often be applied with a lower risk of exacerbating direct conflict. As the only form of military power that covers the full range of military options, from humanitarian assistance to full conventional combat, landpower's flexibility and capabilities help manage both peace and conflict in this region. Should the situation come to conflict, sea and air power would be the primary means of fighting in the South China Sea region. They are what then-Secretary of Defense Ashton Carter bluntly called the "big stick," while transiting the South China Sea aboard the aircraft carrier USS *Theodore Roosevelt*.[6] Landpower is nonetheless important to augment the capabilities found in the other domains through essential direct support to diverse joint military operations, interagency activities, and in its own engagement, deterrence, and strategic combat roles. Perhaps even more important is that the defensive nature of landpower, when applied in this region, is less prone to escalation, while still sending an unequivocal message of resolve to partners and competitors alike. Landpower represents a strong element of "speak softly" engagement to enhance the ability of countries to defend themselves, gives pause to states with aggressive intentions, creates networks that enhance abilities synergistically, and may also break down barriers to misunderstanding—all of which should result in a stabilizing role for U.S. landpower through its proper application in the South China Sea.

To show how U.S. landpower is necessary in stabilizing this contested region during America's strategic rebalance to the Asia-Pacific region, this monograph presents the concept of landpower with its wide-ranging capabilities and its complementary application in the newly articulated concept of the human domain or the human aspects of military operations. The components of landpower are presented, along with how it is a required part of joint operations affecting the air and maritime domains. How landpower supports U.S. interests in the South China Sea sets the stage to then explore landpower's contributions to potential combat operations, through wide area defense and maneuver, deterrence through forward presence, and actual operations. U.S. interests are also complementarily supported through landpower-specific cooperation activities meant to shape beneficial outcomes and assure regional allies and partners, and positively engage possible rivals like China. Associated with these findings are recommendations to better execute land operations in a maritime environment. This monograph will show how landpower is important in a supporting and stabilizing role, even—perhaps especially—in the South China Sea.

LANDPOWER AND THE HUMAN DOMAIN

Throughout history, landpower has been the dominant force available during conflict. With later developments of sea, air, space, and cyberspace power—distinctly articulated by persuasive proponents advocating for fast and technically based victory—the concept of landpower has been taken for granted or simply overlooked. Thus, an overview of landpower, its attributes, capabilities, and components are needed, along with an examination of connections with the human domain and other institutions to gauge their influence on maritime issues.

Landpower is defined by the U.S. Army as "the ability—by threat, force, or occupation—to gain, sustain, and exploit control over land, resources, and people."[7] This official definition, however, seems too focused on landpower's role in a crisis and diminishes its other important contributions to peace and stability. A more apt definition is "the ability in peace, crisis, and war to exert prompt and sustained influence on or from land."[8] This latter definition offers the advantages of broadening landpower's role across the six phases of military operations and widening its reach into each of the environmental domains of military power to enable the synergy of joint operations.[9] Using this latter definition, landpower is viewed from the strategic level, meaning "the application of landpower toward achieving overarching national or multinational . . . security objectives."[10] Landpower advances U.S. interests through all phases of operations, in all environmental domains, and in support of ground and integrated joint operations using personnel and capabilities associated with land forces, as stressed by no one less than USPACOM's Commander Admiral Harry Harris in 2016.[11]

Landpower inherently offers important enduring qualities and attributes that are necessary to any operation in a maritime-dominant environment. For example, landpower can positively control or influence targeted terrain and populations, rather than just deny control to an adversary (as is the mode for air, sea, and cyberspace operations).[12] The corollary to positive control is that landpower is also "temporally durable" in that it can sustain its control far longer than forces in the other domains.[13] Since war and peace are extensions of politics, and politics is a human endeavor, landpower is also a politically decisive force since only it can discriminately and directly influence or control human populations to achieve enduring political outcomes "operat[ing] among populations, not adjacent to them or above them."[14] Landpower is also the most adaptable and comprehensive of the forces—

encompassing missions from peacekeeping and stability operations to major ground combat.[15] With these attributes, "there is no more unmistakable or unambiguous display of American resolve than the highly visible deployment of landpower," as declared jointly by the U.S. Chief of Staff of the Army, Commandant of the Marine Corps, and Commander of U.S. Special Operations Command (USSOCOM).[16] Although the South China Sea region itself lacks land and population, as a semi-enclosed sea fringed by partners, competitors, and large population concentrations that control this region, it remains prime ground to apply the strengths of landpower.

The flexibility and range of roles attributed to landpower are best described by "full spectrum operations," which is an illustrative but older U.S. Army term.[17] Since the end of the Cold War, the Army and Marine Corps have broadened into capability-based (as opposed to threat-based) forces; making them more versatile across the wide spectrum of military operations (see Figure 1).[18] Although the Army best demonstrates this concept through its array and depth of capabilities and more specialized and numerous personnel, this notion also applies to the U.S. Marine Corps, which like the Army has recently been involved in full spectrum operations from stability and special operations to major combat in Iraq and Afghanistan. According to its foundational doctrine, *The Army*, Army Doctrinal Publication (ADP) 1, these full spectrum capabilities enable landpower to:

- Impose the Nation's will on an enemy, by force if necessary.
- Engage to influence, shape, prevent, and deter in any operational environment.
- Establish and maintain a stable environment that sets the conditions for political and economic development.

- Address the consequences of catastrophic events—both natural and man-made—to restore infrastructure and re-establish basic civil services.
- Secure and support bases from which joint forces can influence and dominate the air, land, and maritime domains of an operational environment.[19]

These listed capabilities are exercised through "winning the clash of wills" inherent in human competition in the recently articulated human domain.[20] Each of these capabilities will be explored further in this monograph, since each is of great importance in applying landpower in maritime environments through landpower's combat, deterrence, and engagement operations.

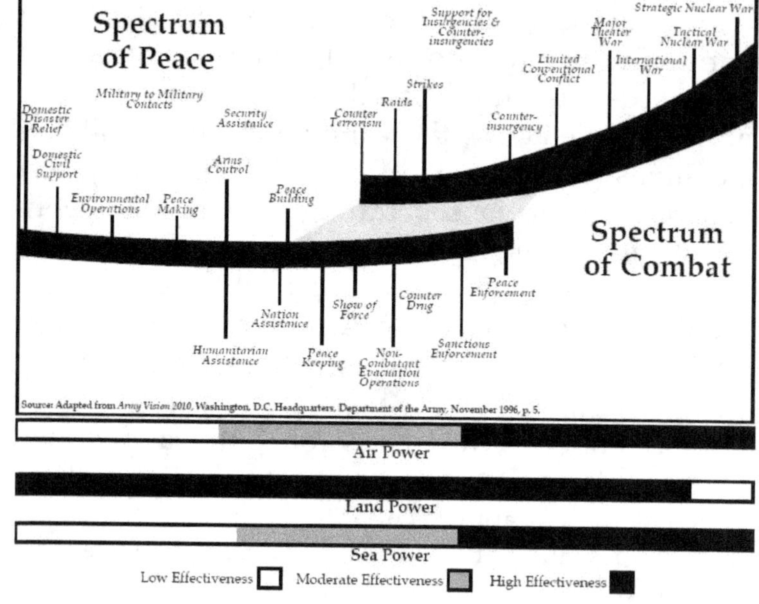

Figure 1. Range of Effectiveness of Military Options.[21]

As nearly all people live on land, and landpower is the predominant force in the land domain, it is also the dominant force in the human domain—such that "the human domain, coupled with the land domain, is the crux for decisive action."[22] This intersection between the land and human domains demonstrates a major role of landpower in a semi-enclosed maritime environment. USSOCOM defines the human domain as "the totality of the physical, cultural and social environments that influence human behavior to the extent that success of any military operation or campaign depends on the application of unique capabilities that are designed to fight and win population-centric conflicts."[23] The British joint doctrine definition, "the totality of the human sphere of activity or knowledge,"[24] parallels the U.S. definition, but is more apt for this analysis because its broader scope may include deterrent and engagement activities that are major landpower contributors to stability using the full spectrum of military operations. Since peace, politics, and war are endeavors in the human domain, they are best conducted person-to-person rather than by technical means, in order to "figur[e] out how other people think so we can influence their actions."[25] As a "conceptualization of the influence that populations have on military operations," this domain and its human factors have long been a part of the "military maneuver space" in terms of culture, religion, history, economic and political relationships, use of technology, and other human attributes, with some detractors complaining that "institutionalizing" the term as a separate human domain unnecessarily muddies a time-tested concept.[26] Use of the term human domain is controversial, even among landpower advocates, and the concept might better be called by its newly coined U.S. Joint Staff J7 term: "human aspects of military operations."[27] Whether a new full-fledged domain or a traditional planning consideration, taking into account that human psychological factors are important in modern military operations, this aspect will play a significant role in U.S. landpower in maritime environments, especially in military engagement activities and preventing "population centric-conflict."[28]

After examining landpower, its attributes, and its influence within the land and human domains, understanding the composition of landpower forces are helpful to establish their importance in the South China Sea disputes. U.S. landpower is a triad of land forces from the Army, Marine Corps, and Special Operations Command (SOCOM), including their reserve components, numbering over one million members, although that may change under U.S. President Donald Trump's administration.[29] "U.S. ground forces provide expeditionary (especially . . . [U.S. Marine Corps]) and sustained (especially . . . [U.S. Army]) capability needed to deter or defeat aggression,"[30] and USSOCOM's core competency is its high-impact, low-footprint combat effectiveness and persuasive engagement within the human domain.[31] The Army claims the core war fighting competencies of combined arms maneuver, wide area security, and special operations—each detailed in this monograph—which collectively constitute its offensive, defensive, and stability operations. In support of other military services, the Army also claims seven enabling competencies that serve joint and combined operations, also to be covered in detail.[32] Like the Army, the Marine Corps operates in the land and human domains, differing in its reliance on the maritime domain as its operational base in order to be "the right force in the right place at the right time."[33] These rapid response capabilities can "shape the environment, and set conditions to deploy the full capabilities of the Joint Force and other elements of National Power," but Marine operations lack the sustainability and political decisiveness of the U.S. Army.[34] Special Operations Forces (SOF) are not a separate service, but draw forces from the U.S. Army SOCOM, U.S. Marine Corps Forces SOCOM, and specialized elements of the U.S. Air Force and Navy.[35] Joint Publication (JP) 3-05, *Special Operations*, states that:

> Special operations require unique modes of employment, tactics, techniques, procedures, and equipment. They are often conducted in hostile, denied, or politically and/or diplomatically sensitive environments, and are characterized by one or more of the following: time-sensitivity, clandestine or covert nature, low visibility, work with or through indigenous forces, greater requirements for regional orientation and cultural expertise, and a higher degree of risk.[36]

SOFs are even lighter, faster, and more focused than Marines, but also less able to sustain themselves.[37] In the South China Sea region, SOFs are especially important for "training, advising, and assisting . . . foreign forces, enabling them to support their governments' security and stability,"[38] and are well suited for operations in the "gray zone" of conflict between full war and peace.[39] During the fighting in Iraq and Afghanistan, SOF and conventional land forces attained an "unprecedented level of interdependence and cooperation" that will continue to serve the United States well in its pursuit of national objectives.[40]

One last aspect of landpower must be emphasized: landpower does not stand alone but is fully integrated and interdependent with forces of the other domains as practiced within U.S. joint doctrine.[41] Expectations in modern joint operations are no longer for the military services to be just interoperable, but also interdependent, defined as "the deliberate reliance of one armed service on the capabilities of another armed service,"[42] meaning that the military services "will depend upon each other for the performance of the majority of the[ir] roles, missions, and tasks."[43] This results in the "seamless application of combat power between domains," or "cross-domain synergy."[44] Thus, U.S. land forces support and operate in synergy with sea, air, cyber, and space forces under a joint commander (i.e., the commander of USPACOM or a delegated subordinate), and also integrate with the activities of other government agencies (the interagency in "unified action") and in multinational (combined) efforts.[45] Under these circumstances, the U.S. Army contributes to joint operations to: "(1) shape the security environment; (2) set the theater; and (3) project national power . . . [as well as] conduct: (4) combined arms maneuver; (5) wide area security . . . and (7) special operations."[46] In a predominately maritime region, some landpower capabilities that support joint operations, as covered in this monograph, include logistics and sustainment support, wide area defense, maneuver from the sea, air and sea control from the land, engineering and civil action, and the creation of a secure environment.[47] As lighter, more combat-oriented forces, special operations and Marine Corps forces provide much less enabling support to other forces, instead, needing support for their own long-term activities. Landpower's support to joint operations is especially relevant in the South China Sea, since its other core warfighting competencies are clipped by the far-flung maritime environment.

Even in a sea- and air-dominant environment, landpower's broad operational and strong support capabilities in pursuit of increasingly interdependent joint and unified operations make it an indispensable element in attaining U.S. interests. Landpower may be the most decisive force through persistent control of terrain and populations in the land and human domains. Land forces are also the most flexible and versatile force through full spectrum operations, making it essential at all levels of military operations, from peacetime engagement to major combat—especially the ability to understand, engage, and influence people through the activities of SOF and, increasingly, Army and Marine forces. Landpower's capabilities are crucial for attaining the United States' national security interests of peace and stability in maritime environments.

LANDPOWER'S SUPPORT TO U.S. INTERESTS IN THE SOUTH CHINA SEA

The United States' national interests are simple, broad, and long-standing. They ensure:
- The security of the United States, its citizens, and U.S. allies and partners;
- A strong, innovative, and growing U.S. economy in an open international economic system that promotes opportunity and prosperity;
- Respect for universal values at home and around the world; and
- A rules-based international order advanced by U.S. leadership that promotes peace, security, and opportunity through stronger cooperation to meet global challenges.[48]

Each of these interests is directly supported by U.S. military forces as outlined in the DoD's QDR report and other supporting documents.[49] For example, the 2012 *National Defense Strategy* established the "rebalance toward the Asia-Pacific region," emphasizing support to existing alliances and expanding cooperation with emerging partners, making the first national interest a prime task for U.S. landpower in the South China Sea region through its strategic roles of combat, deterrence, and engagement.[50] Deterrence, through U.S. military forces and its allies and partners, also supports the economy and an open international system by ensuring free movement through the world's busiest waterway and the well-being of a major region's economy. Landpower addresses this interest by preventing intimidation, promoting internal stability, and building relationships in the region.[51] Landpower is especially adept at reinforcing respect for universal values through military-to-military shaping and engagement activities with other forces in Southeast Asia, as will also be shown.[52] Finally, landpower's presence promotes stability and security by reassuring friends through security cooperation activities and engaging adversaries beneficially—with additional positive effects from engagement bestowed to the other national interests as well.[53] American values and interests in the region have remained consistent for decades, but the importance of landpower in their pursuit has increased in both its harder and softer forms.

These U.S. interests, through the military and landpower's strategic roles, are manifest in 10 primary missions assigned to the U.S. Armed Forces by the DoD.[54] Around the South China Sea, landpower, with forces from the other domains, directly supports the combat missions to:

- Deter and Defeat Aggression
- Project Power Despite Anti-Access Area Denial [A2AD] Challenges[55]

Under deterrence and contingency operations, land-power:

- [Performs] Counterterrorism and Irregular Warfare
- Provide[s] A Stabilizing Presence
- Conduct[s] Stability and Counterinsurgency Operations
- Conduct[s] Humanitarian, Disaster Relief, and Other Operations[56]

Engagement activities with partners and rivals build understanding, cooperation, capabilities, and confidence, useful on their own, but that also strengthens deterrence and combat abilities.[57] To fulfill these missions, USPACOM's strategy in essence:

> USPACOM protects and defends, in concert with other U.S. Government agencies, the territory of the United States, its people, and its interests. With allies and partners, USPACOM is committed to enhancing stability in the Asia-Pacific region by promoting security cooperation, encouraging peaceful development, responding to contingencies, deterring aggression, and, when necessary, fighting to win. This approach is based on partnership, presence, and military readiness.[58]

The subordinate landpower headquarters of U.S. Army Pacific Command (USARPAC), Marine Corps Forces Pacific (MARFORPAC), and Special Operations Command Pacific (SOCPAC) address the USPACOM commander's intent by supporting access to common domains, strengthening alliances and partnerships through security cooperation and engagement, enhancing landpower's forward presence and posture in the region, sustaining force projection into the region, assisting others against terrorism and during disasters, and being ready to fight and win.[59] Despite the apparent environmental limitations the region imposes on land forces, landpower directly supports national objectives in the South China Sea region along with the other U.S. Government agencies, services, and international partners and allies.

Where U.S. interests overlap with the interests of other states in the region, landpower may also support and be a welcome addition to the mutual goals of stability and security. Even a potential competitor like China shares interests with the United States as cited in the 2010 U.S. *National Security Strategy* (NSS), which directs U.S. Government efforts to "pursue a positive, constructive, and comprehensive relationship with China," a tone that was continued in the 2015 NSS.[60] Former Secretary of Defense Leon Panetta noted that both countries have a stake in codependent prosperity and security in the region and thus need a productive bilateral relationship, which with time will probably be adopted by President Trump's administration, as did initially "tough-on-China" former U.S. Presidents Ronald Reagan, Bill Clinton, and George W. Bush within a year or two of taking office.[61] A peaceful regional environment allows the Chinese Government to focus on its "national goal . . . to build a moderately prosperous society and achieve the great rejuvenation of the Chinese people by 2050," which is key to maintaining its legitimacy; they have also used bilateral, multilateral, and institutional engagements to achieve some common goals.[62] Potential and actual military-to-military exchanges of mutual interest with China emanating from landpower cover counterterrorism and other transnational threat initiatives, humanitarian and disaster response, peacekeeping, professional education, and building personal contacts that are indispensable to preventing misperception and building cooperation, especially important during times of tension (as is covered in more detail later in this monograph).[63] Peaceful development through successful engagement, both military and with the other elements of national power, over common interests with China benefits all sides, and landpower is a robust component in achieving it through security cooperation efforts that "help ward off miscalculation and war."[64]

Although USPACOM is actively building military-to-military relationships with China, it must also balance a credible military deterrence and fighting ability against it because this complex relationship is also one of rivalry and diverging interests.[65] Secretary of Defense James Mattis identified China as one of the three greatest challenges to the United States since World War II, remarking that relations with China would require special management, especially with respect to the South China Sea,[66] since many analysts believe that China wants to dominate the region and deny influence there to the United States.[67] The Chinese military strategy to achieve this:

> 'Active Defense,' states that the PRC [People's Republic of China] will never take aggressive offensive action outside its territory, but is prepared to defend its territory [including] . . . territorial waters and airspace . . . [and] safeguarding its maritime rights and interests.[68]

Active Defense allows the preemptive use of force but avoids involvement in major wars when possible.[69] China's 2009 reaffirmation of the U-Shaped line in the South China Sea is part of this strategy to control its claimed national space, although it was not recognized by the international Permanent Court of Arbitration in The Hague in its 2016 ruling and is actively contested by its neighbors—China's aggressive enforcement of its claims has led to clashes.[70] The U.S. response to this has not been a Cold War-like policy of containment, as asserted by the Chinese, but a more nuanced channel to funnel China's rise in power and use of influence toward internationally acceptable methods and goals.[71] American diplomat Zalmay Khalilzad describes the American response as "congagement," in which containment and confrontation are used with engagement to affect a range of activities that a peacetime U.S. military may perform to influence China's rise. This results in three possible U.S.-China security relationships in the South China Sea: first, they may "establish a security partnership designed to protect common interests; second, they remain security competitors with an ambiguous relationship; or third, they become adversarial."[72] U.S. landpower's ability to project power from the land and sea as well as engage peacefully on security issues is part of this "congagement" mix to channel Chinese actions and its ultimate rise in power in a way that benefits U.S., Chinese, and neighbors' interests.[73]

The United States and the region's powers need each other's support to achieve their shared interests of preventing conflict and developing stability and prosperity in the South China Sea region, especially for freedom of navigation and access to the resources of this regional commons.[74] The Southeast

Asian states have traditionally been wary of China's growing military capability and assertiveness, which have put each at an economic, political, and military disadvantage, but these states have been unable to coalesce or effectively counter China on their own.[75] China's antagonism sometimes pushes these Southeast Asian states to seek more U.S. diplomatic and military presence to balance the Chinese hegemon.[76] China's coercion is most recently seen in the "coercive gradualism" or small "gray zone" advances of dredging reefs into artificial islands and militarizing them along with advanced A2AD capability and belligerent maritime confrontations.[77] China also co-opts these states through economic dependence as a major trading partner, with investments and developments through instruments like China's new Asian Infrastructure Investment Bank, and other interests affecting all, such as energy security and counterterrorism. Weak U.S. leadership and presence in the region may have led Philippine President Rodrigo Duterte to seek rapprochement and more balanced relations with a previously antagonistic China.

Even these beneficial actions worry some regional leaders for the dependence they foster in an unequal hub-and-spoke system with China dominating the center.[78] For that reason, the expansion of U.S. defense and security ties would be welcome. U.S. landpower can play a reassuring role for these partners through countering transnational security threats, natural disaster operations, professionalization of forces, information sharing, building partner military capacity and interoperability in missions from peacekeeping to combat, and the simple presence of U. S. forces, which help partner states to better face internal and external threats.[79] Committing U.S. landpower to the region is a strong indication of U.S. determination for partners and allies' security; but regional partners balance their diplomacy between China and the United States, as they are not fully convinced of America's commitment to pivot to Asia, or how this may effect Chinese behavior in the long-term.[80] For instance, how far will the United States support Filipino actions on Scarborough Shoal after the South China Sea ruling by the Permanent Court of Arbitration?[81] Common interests and a desire for strategic balance led USARPAC's former commander, General Vincent Brooks, to observe, "Many of the countries in the region look to the United States as kind of an honest broker and a big brother," to balance the perceived dominating tendencies by China.[82]

U.S. landpower's traits and capabilities may be the best suited among the military services to perform the broad strategic roles of "bolstering defense of allies and deterring aggression; promoting regional security and stability through security cooperation; and ameliorating the growing United States-China security dilemma" in support of mutually shared goals.[83] Landpower plays a prime role because of its inherent and influential advantages with the militaries of the Southeast Asian littoral. Even in this maritime-rich environment, few states can afford effective air or naval forces. The lack of air or naval forces results in regional military structures dominated by land forces which can best address these states' most important security requirements, which are often land-based, "giving army-army contacts greater weight in military, political, and security affairs."[84] In 2017, the Chiefs of the Armed Forces of China, Taiwan, Malaysia, the Philippines, Vietnam, Indonesia, and Brunei were army officers; and the army was the largest and most influential force in each of these states as well.[85] At the much lower squad-level, soldiers and marines of the region also have more in common with U.S. land forces than their counterparts have with the highly sophisticated U.S. Air Force or Navy.[86] Thus, assistance from the world's most credible army, marine, and SOF are often well-received in the region, and these land-force-to-land-force contacts greatly enhance the other forms of U.S. national power.[87]

The physical environment makes U.S. land forces a more influential and welcome stabilizer in the South China Sea region, ironically for similar reasons why landpower is often overlooked there. In the insular and littoral geography of Southeast Asia, the classic picture of U.S. land forces massing troops and maneuvering over swaths of land is restrained, forcing it instead to employ its supporting missions, which present U.S. landpower as a more defensive and less threatening presence to a rival since its capabilities in the region are distinct from offensive ones, while still reassuring partners.[88] Forward deploying ground troops into a contentious region is the most tangible signal possible of U.S. resolve and commitment by a casualty-adverse American public.[89] Land forces working in small units within the human domain may be less visible and thus more politically acceptable while discreetly operating close to native forces and reassuring allies with their ability to hold ground.[90] Land forces are well suited to perform manpower intensive activities of mutual interest to partners in non-threatening areas like disaster response, development missions, and transnational crime while supporting a U.S. interagency partner through civic action.[91] Such engagement reassures by strengthening the long-term stability and legitimacy of Southeast Asian partners and by giving an American presence a softer, collaborative hue, while still being able to act as a deterrent in the region.

Landpower cooperating with allies and partners in this way may help to allay China's perception of the threat of U.S. forces deployed around the South China Sea littorals.[92] China's relationship with U.S. air and sea power, however, is framed by the Air-Sea Battle concept that stresses the second part of their "cooperate-compete" relationship, and although a necessary part of a comprehensive American strategy, Air-Sea Battle entails danger and risk that needs to be balanced by other approaches.[93] Former Secretary of Defense Carter's earlier reference to the "big stick" is balanced by a "speak softly" engagement of which U.S. landpower is the main proponent in a (more, but not entirely) cooperative military relationship with China.[94] The USARPAC commander once described land forces as the "good cop, cooperating with its Chinese counterparts on such mutually beneficial missions as disaster relief."[95] Such a U.S. landpower presence and relationship may benefit all sides by "mitigating some of the worst fears . . . over China's rise . . . [while] China might welcome a pacifying role played by the United States vis-à-vis aggressive tendencies of American allies."[96] Unlike sea and air power, U.S. landpower does not challenge any of China's current main objectives in the region—such as control of the South China Sea islands, historic rights to its resources, and protection of sea lanes and the homeland—nor does it engage in the most immediate source of friction—close proximity surveillance from China's claimed waters.[97] With these inherent advantages, U.S. land forces may engage closer with China and the Southeast Asian states to continue to reassure, build confidence, and bring stability to their overall relationships.

Land forces are an important and adaptive contributor in support of mutual U.S., partner, and competitor interests around the South China Sea through U.S. landpower's inherent strengths and capabilities. If the United States is to channel tensions in the region toward internationally acceptable forms of growth, prosperity, stability, and security, U.S. landpower holds an outsized influence, because: land-force-to-land-force contact is the dominate influence in this region's military structure; the less threatening defensive nature of U.S. landpower in the area; and its ability to play the "good cop" through engagement. USARPAC, SOCPAC, and MARFORPAC are dual-missioned for peacetime engagement and combat, for instance:

> Engaging the theater and working alongside partners is USARPAC's first line of effort in a theater campaign support plan designed to enable the command—*by, with, or through allies and partners*—to deter aggression, build capacity, and assure USPACOM success [italics in original].[98]

This soft role for land forces is summarized succinctly as "day-to-day engagement [that] plays a fundamental role in shaping the strategic and operational security environment . . . vital to communicating intent and influencing others in the region to address shared interests."[99] From this firm grounding of what and who landpower is, how it supports American security interests around the South China Sea littoral, and its special influence there, how this is accomplished through landpower's capabilities is addressed next.

CAPABILITIES OF LANDPOWER IN THE SOUTH CHINA SEA

The balance of cooperation and confrontation among China, the United States, and Southeast Asian countries is a delicate one. The Council of Foreign Affairs' *Preventive Priorities Survey 2017* categorizes the possibility of conflict in the East and South China Seas as potentially high in impact, if low in likelihood, while other commentators forecast confrontation between a rising and established world power.[100] For this possibility, U.S. joint land forces must be prepared for their combat role in defending U.S. and allied interests, and supporting air and sea power in their roles, "if for no other reason than to deter [war]."[101] Prevention or deterrence of conflict is a second major role of landpower using its presence and capabilities to reassure partners and to help stabilize against internal and external political, developmental, environmental disaster, and military challenges.[102] Former U.S. President Barack Obama's administration worked under the premise that conflict with China was possible, but not inevitable, thus necessitating strong U.S. alliances and military capability. Despite its early hawkish announcements, this may develop to be the Trump administration's policy, since Secretary of State Rex Tillerson's core foreign policy belief appears be that the United States needs to reassert itself as a means of deterrence to reassure Asian allies and to counter what Trump advisers Peter Navarro and Alexander Gray described as Obama's policy of speaking loudly but "carrying a small stick."[103] The three strategic roles of U.S. landpower—shape by assuring friends and restraining adversaries through engagement; prevent or deter conflict by denying an aggressor its objectives through presenting credible combat forces; and win by compelling an enemy and dominating decisively when committed—are an efficient framework used here to analyze landpower's capabilities.[104] Although parsed in this analysis, all three strategic roles are interdependent upon each other and other services and agencies for success. This section presents landpower's capabilities in terms of its indispensable support to joint operations, its combat roles of wide area security and maneuver in a semi-enclosed maritime environment, its contributions to deterrence through a tangible forward presence and through crisis and contingency operations, and landpower's premier engagement abilities to build military partner capacity, reassure allies, and engage adversaries.

One of landpower's greatest but most overlooked contributions to stability and security in the South China Sea is its foundational enabling support to joint forces. Because these support functions enable activities for all of the forces of air, sea, and land in their strategic roles, they will be presented before the specific role analysis of landpower that follows. As the largest and most diverse in capabilities, the U.S. Army features prominently as the DoD executive agent or lead service for a variety of joint combat support and sustainment enabling competencies directed by DoD and USPACOM.[105] One of the Army's directed responsibilities, as assigned by DoD Directive 5100.01, is to "provide logistics to joint operations and campaigns" or set the theater for joint use of U.S. military forces and other agencies of the U.S. Government and international forces.[106] The Army's 8th Theater Sustainment Command provides expertise and depth in these functions that "gives [U.S.] forces extraordinary endurance" in an efficient manner "to campaign for months and years, often in harsh environments."[107] Even in a maritime or air dispute that lasted more than a week, U.S. military services' interdependence would require U.S. Army logistical support for sustaining dispersed airbases or the opening of ports and airfields.[108] This operational Army task entails deliberate or forcible entry and theater opening to allow the "reception, staging, and onward movement" of joint or combined forces arriving in theater for engagement, deterrence, or combat activities.[109] Once open, the Army ensures that logistics like food, fuel, ammunition, and medical support are distributed to the military services and civilian agencies like the U.S. Agency for International Development (USAID) through its port operations, helicopter lift, and long-haul trucking.[110] Although the U.S. Army usually sustains joint forces when deployed, U.S. Marine forces can sustain themselves ashore and logistically support other joint forces for a limited period.[111] Other unsung Army enabling support to the joint forces includes command, control, and communications. The U.S. Army is the most experienced and forthcoming of the military services in establishing joint task force (JTF) headquarters for theater commanders by setting up and integrating communication systems for all joint, interagency, and combined forces, and providing tailorable and scalable higher echelon division and corps headquarters as the command structure for JTFs.[112] The U.S. Army also has a major medical capability in the Asia-Pacific region, including the deployable 18th Medical Command, offering preventive care, pandemic response, medical combat care, and intraregional medical transport for the joint forces.[113] These and other services, like intelligence, are the foundation the U.S. Army lays for joint force operations in the South China Sea region. However, the potential A2AD and coercive gradualism threats around the region mean that these normally rear-area services are not always safe from attack and require other landpower capabilities to defend them and U.S. joint forces.

Landpower's Combat and Compel Capabilities.

This monograph has made the case that, although unsought and unlikely, conflict could occur in the South China Sea region, and any combat involving the United States by necessity would involve U.S. landpower. In this semi-enclosed maritime environment, however, some aspects of landpower's combat capabilities are restrained, while other capabilities are accentuated. The Army's foundational doctrine ADP-1 categorizes landpower combat as "the ability to impose the Nation's will on an enemy, by force if necessary."[114] This is summed up by landpower's strategic role of "win," in which it "must be ready to win decisively and dominantly when committed."[115] The caveat "by force if necessary" recognizes a second option of compelling an adversary with threatening or adverse expectations without an actual use of force in achieving national interests against an enemy's will. Even if combat in the region is unlikely, the credibility of U.S. land forces in waging it is very important to deter conflict, to shape circumstances, and to reassure allies of their safety, security, and own capabilities. On this point, the retired Chief of the Australian Army, Lieutenant General David Morrison, observed that U.S. landpower's "ability to shape and prevent is a direct reflection of [its] ability to compel . . . if you do not have the ability to win as a ground force, people are less likely to listen to you."[116] U.S. landpower's most important contributions to compel and fight in the South China Sea arena are associated mainly with the U.S. Army conventional forces' core competencies of wide area security and combined arms maneuver, shared with the U.S. Marine Corps.[117] This section addresses U.S. landpower's specific combat contributions germane to the South China Sea by analyzing its DoD directed responsibilities to the joint force, including missile forces to "interdict enemy air, sea, and space forces . . . from the land"; to "conduct airborne, air assault, and amphibious operations"; and to ensure wide area security, which will start this section's analysis.[118]

Wide area security is one of the most important combat capabilities of landpower and a core competency of the U.S. Army. It is the "application of the elements of combat power in unified action to protect populations, forces, infrastructure, and activities."[119] The effort to protect an area from hostile threats can be done cooperatively with host nation forces, in contested areas during counterinsurgency operations, or coercively by seizing terrain and defending it (the latter scenarios are explained more in the deterrent and maneuver sections respectively).[120] In the South China Sea region, U.S. Army and Marine forces are particularly adept at enhancing regional security using their diverse combat support capabilities against threats posed to land-based joint and partner forces.[121] The most numerous forces in a combatant commander's area of responsibility (AOR) are often land forces. Consequently, they are often assigned to wide area security through the concurrent use of the branches of landpower from infantry to engineers, intelligence, civil affairs, and aviation, to name just a few.[122] An example of these missions includes hardening vulnerable wireless communications with well-buried landlines using communication and engineer troops to counter foreign intelligence intercepts and missile attacks.[123] Military police and intelligence forces work together to defend against attacks of sabotage or insurgency on high-value assets like aircraft or headquarters, as was inflicted on U.S. forces during their involvement in the American-Vietnam War—a situation easily repeated in the coercive gradualism tactics practiced today in lower intensity conflicts.[124] Within the intricate coasts and rivers of the region, internal security and protection may also be enhanced through the re-emerging concept of Mobile Riverine Forces that integrate a Marine Air-Ground Task Force (MAGTF) with a Navy river assault group and host nation forces to patrol and pacify restive areas.[125] Although an important capability for shallow water maneuver in this region, this requirement remains unfunded.[126] As the most numerous and specialized troops for such missions and a well-practiced and proffered command and control (C2) capability for land control operations, a land force commander is often designated the Joint Security Coordinator for the Joint Security Area (JSA) that protects friendly territory and infrastructure in a designated, usually rear, area. U.S. land forces would probably be assigned most JSA duties if one were again set up in Southeast Asia.[127] In addition, joint land forces enabled by U.S. Army civil affairs units often provide essential support during natural or man-made disasters, and during routine visits and exchanges they often work "to improve conditions over time and subsequently increase local and regional stability."[128] These are a sampling of the many necessary, but unglamorous tasks, which usually befall joint land forces to protect friendly forces, populations, territories, and infrastructure when needed by allies and partners. Also part of wide area security is the defense of territory and people by ensuring air and sea defense from the land capabilities, discussed next.

One proven function of landpower, as assigned by DoD to the U.S. Army, is its ability to defend against air and missile attacks using land-based radar and missile systems integrated under the joint force air component commander.[129] In the South China Sea region, forward U.S. and friendly bases are vulnerable to preemptive air and missile strikes from China's burgeoning A2AD system, meant to disrupt concentrated in-place or reinforcing U.S. and partner logistics and combat forces on land and at sea.[130] For Southeast Asian countries, Chinese A2AD systems also have the potential for political coercion and to contest access to the South China Sea. Deployed U.S. air and missile defenses, commanded by the 94th Army Air and Missile Defense Command, are a partial counter to Chinese coercive gradualism.[131] American partners and allies value these capabilities based on proven engagement against aircraft, cruise, and ballistic missiles; high system availability rate; concealment through road mobility; and, a relatively low public profile as defensive systems in host countries. Tactical anti-air and anti-missile capabilities are delivered by the Patriot missile system; while inside and outside the atmosphere, ballistic missile intercepts are conducted at a greater range by the Theater High Altitude Area Defense (THAAD) system.[132] While the first operational deployment of a THAAD system in 2013 to protect forces in the U.S. territory of Guam seems to be permanent, none of the Southeast Asian states has a similar capability. Even if invited to use Antonio Bautista Air Base (AB), a recently authorized temporary facility for U.S. forces on the western-most Philippine island of Palawan, THAAD's range of 200 km would cover only a few of the most eastern Spratly Island features (and hardly any of the disputed oil-rich Reed Bank) and would not cover Scarborough Shoal from the nearest Philippine coastline, nor any features from Malaysia's Borneo coast. The Patriot's range is even shorter, limiting both systems to point defense.[133] Improvements are in the process for each, with a future Patriot already successfully tested against tactical ballistic missiles, and a proposed THAAD-Extended Range potentially defending an area 9-12 times its current capabilities.[134]

Besides range, other weaknesses of both systems are their expense compared to the threats they counter, and a limited number of units to fill the much larger worldwide demand for them.[135] Only 15 Patriot battalions and 6 THAAD batteries are operational in the entire army—eventually growing to 7 THAAD batteries, although a requirement for at least 9 batteries exists in the fiscally constrained budget. At the very least, U.S. bases on the southern Japanese island of Okinawa should also field Patriot and THAAD batteries.[136] Additional air defense capability may be available through the Navy's future Aegis Ashore System and those already aboard ships, but ship capability is also in short-supply and meant to defend the fleet, and which military service would employ a land-based Aegis remains contentious.[137] To address these and other problems, a U.S. Senate bill intends to fund a "comprehensive operational assessment of a potential future role for U.S. ground forces in the island chains of the western Pacific in creating anti-access/area denial (A2/AD) capabilities in cooperation with host nations."[138] As witnessed by China's objections to the deployment of THAAD to South Korea to defend against a North Korean menace, China would likely also object to its deployment to defend U.S. partners around the South China Sea. As part of landpower's wide area security role of defending defined areas and populations to reassure allies and protect forces and infrastructure, the limited range and small number make U.S. anti-air and anti-missile systems deployed to the South China Sea arena truly defensive systems against intimidation and for force protection, and not one of force projection.[139]

Another vital wide area security mission that U.S. landpower could play in the South China Sea revives the role of maritime control from the land. "Coastal defense was a core role of the U.S. Army in the 1800s and later, in the first half of the 1900s of the Marine Corps," and is well suited as a modern mission in semi-enclosed maritime environments.[140] *The Army Operating Concept, 2020-2040* outlines the U.S. Army's role in operating from the land domain in support of the air and maritime domains as part of the cross-domain synergy that complements the Air-Sea Battle concept.[141] Modernized long-range anti-ship missiles employed by existing Army missile batteries could provide a new role for landpower that offers advantages. These include better hardened and dispersed assets than ship-based systems, increased effectiveness through greater available firepower, less cost as a deployed force, and when "fielded on a country's sovereign territory, mak[es] a preemptive strike against them a significant escalation."[142] In this role, landpower complements air and sea power by maintaining near constant presence and creating options for friendly forces through bottlenecks and greater freedom of maneuver.[143] This capability does not now exist, however, with U.S. Army and Marine Corps commanders reluctant to assume such a positional defense role again, choosing instead to emphasize maneuver capabilities during shrinking budgets.[144] Some Army officials, however, support use of land-adapted RGM-84 Harpoons or the future development of a hypersonic anti-ship missile system for such a mission.[145] Both Vietnam and Japan are developing shore-based anti-ship capabilities to match China's A2AD, which offer cooperation opportunities to U.S. land forces. To increase allied interoperability and decrease acquisition time, the U.S. Army could adopt the Japanese or another land-based system. Using an allied system would "also promote partnered A2AD networks among friendly nations" to act both as a stronger deterrent and a more effective weapon.[146] With a range of around 125 km, a land-based Harpoon system would remain a defensive weapon. However, should U.S. or friendly land forces employ a weapon with a greater range, similar to the 400 km Chinese YJ-62 anti-ship cruise missile already deployed to the Paracel Islands,[147] they could cover much of the Spratly Islands from Philippine shores and—in conjunction with a deployment to Vietnam—contest sea lanes across much of the South China Sea while also covering most of the Paracel Islands.[148] Former Defense Secretary Ashton Carter supported a hypervelocity projectile, which is a "precision-guided shell that can be fired from traditional artillery and naval cannons to give vastly greater range against a wide variety of targets, including ships at sea and potentially even incoming cruise missiles."[149] Admiral Harris, USPACOM Commander, envisions the use of "ground-based artillery to put 'steel' into the deep, blue sea—emplacing intelligent sea mines to restrict movement in the maritime domain."[150] Such capabilities pose an A2AD dilemma for China, as the United States is "merely trying to defend our allies. It's the Chinese who have to come out."[151] An anti-ship mission still fits within the definition of wide area security, and adopting this concept in the South China Sea area has bipartisan support in the U.S. Congress, which requested a report "as to the feasibility, utility, and options for mobile, land-based systems to provide anti-ship fires."[152] China would object to the deployment of land-based coastal defense systems to the South China Sea; however, they would be reassuring for allies as the formation of a friendly A2AD system, a counter to Chinese militarization of the sea, and could make air and sea control from the land an "immovable anvil to the mobile hammer of the Air Force, Navy and Marines."[153]

A third method by which U.S. landpower may counter Chinese power projection in the South China Sea is through land-based attack missiles, which could complicate aggressive Chinese actions by creating a contested no man's "land," forcing China to deploy defensive systems, not just offensive ones.[154] Mobile surface-to-surface missiles can target small, militarized land features in a semi-enclosed maritime environment. Land attack missiles act not only as a "sword" against enemy forces on land, but also as a "shield" by suppressing an enemy's ability to project power, which, along with air and sea defenses, enable friendly entry operations into the theater, and air and sea power to "form a mobile reserve behind the land defenses."[155] U.S. Army forces currently use the MGM-140 Army Tactical Missile System (ATACMS), which is a proven precision strike system against stationary or slow moving land targets at ranges up to 300 km.[156] Using ATACMS, an expeditionary force (EF) in the Philippines could range the eastern half of the Spratly Islands and Scarborough Shoals and just touch the Paracel Islands or China's Hainan Dao from Vietnam. Like U.S. anti-air and anti-ship missile systems, the range and availability of current land attack missiles categorize this as a short-range suppression system, and so it remains in the wide area security mission. A missile system that increased ranges to 500 km would cover all of the Spratly Islands from the Philippines and all of the Paracels and Hainan Dao from Vietnam.[157] Former Secretary Carter also used the U.S. Navy's reprogramming of its Tomahawk cruise missile to target moving ships at sea as an example for modifying ATACMS in the same way. Further enhancing U.S. capabilities is an in-development joint battle network linking sensor, C2, and fires from each of the military services so that information may be passed across systems and services to assist each other against air, sea, and land targets.[158] Enhanced range and overlapping missile systems would be a direct threat to China's Hainan Dao, but could counter the escalation of missile systems already in place in the Paracel and Spratly Islands.[159]

Another method of projecting power in a maritime environment is through the second of landpower's core competencies: movement and maneuver used "to achieve a position of relative advantage" over a threat.[160] The lack of maneuver by land is what some people consider when diminishing the influence of landpower in the South China Sea, but amphibious and air maneuver has had successful historic precedents in the Pacific region.[161] The essential purpose for Air-Sea Battle is to enable maneuver for air, sea, and land operations in the region to effect "what happens on the land area of the littoral environment."[162] Amphibious maneuver is a core capability of the U.S.

Marine Corps, under the key Marine Corps tasks of power projection and littoral maneuver, but one also assigned by DoD to the U.S. Army and SOF, all with support of the U.S. Navy.[163] The amphibious role manifests in Air-Sea Battle as "seizing and defending advanced bases, particularly remote islands" to control the sea and air space around them in order to conduct follow-on operations.[164] For this mission, the Marines use the combined arms MAGTF, consisting of ground, air, and logistical support elements.[165] Unlike historic amphibious missions, however, the Marines employ the modern Seabasing Joint Integrated Concept, by which supporting ships are located over the horizon, projecting forces with a reduced logistics footprint directly onto or up to 240 miles beyond the beach to create a lodgment or staging area. The advantage of this ship-to-objective maneuver concept is: its flexibility in employing 3,000 marines and 15-days of supply with greater "speed, access, and persistence"; its ability to avoid enemy concentrations or nodes; that it requires less prepositioned afloat or logistical assets; and that it is not necessarily dependent upon use of vulnerable foreign sovereign fixed-facilities.[166] Examples of combat seabasing and ship-to-objective maneuver are the insertion of marines from the Arabian Sea directly into combat positions in Afghanistan in 2001 and during Operation IRAQI FREEDOM in 2003.[167] Although it entails significant force structure changes, the U.S. Army's Training and Doctrine Command (TRADOC) is also implementing seabasing to revamp its mostly atrophied amphibious capability.[168] For instance, the Army is currently training its helicopter pilots to operate from U.S. Navy ships at sea, and is making a priority acquisition for about two dozen multipurpose landing craft, the Maneuver Support Vessel (Light), replacing the Vietnam War era Landing Craft Mechanized or "Mike Boat."[169]

The second form of landpower maneuver in this prevailing maritime realm is from the air, using conventional Army and SOF, which, like amphibious operations, are built upon the Army's core competency of combined arms maneuver to gain access and project power.[170] Air operations originate from land bases and are transported directly to their objectives by the U.S. Air Force or Army Aviation. Airborne (parachute) and air assault (helicopter) operations are forms of forcible-entry to seize key remote, peripheral, or vulnerable rear areas by deploying quickly and stealthily, avoiding high threat areas, using scalable forces, and maneuvering to achieve surprise that, along with other offensive options, complicates an enemy's defense and gives the joint commander more options to take the initiative.[171] The U.S. Army's former chief futurist, Lieutenant General H.R. McMaster, observed:

> this is not just about fires, it's about maneuver . . . You can't just stand at a distance and shoot, you have to keep moving . . . constantly presenting [the enemy] with multiple dilemmas. We're working very closely with the Marine Corps in particular on future maneuver by dispersed yet mutually supporting units.[172]

Despite the advantages and modern capabilities of landpower's current air and amphibious forcible entry operations, their use is fraught with risk in a dangerous A2AD environment. First, after many years of concentrating on counterinsurgency in Iraq and Afghanistan, the forcible entry and combined-arms skills of marines and soldiers are unexercised, and much work is still needed in updating and increasing equipment, exercises, and doctrine to survive in the exposed and threat dense A2AD environment of some semi-enclosed maritime environments.[173] The capability of partner countries is even weaker, as to limit any combined maneuver operations without much needed improvement in capabilities.[174] China's imposing air-, sea-, and land-based A2AD systems that implement its Area Control Strategy were assembled to challenge other countries' control in the region out to the second island chain, making vulnerable U.S. entry and partner country operations by threatening facilities, transportation systems, and lodgments as far as Guam and the Marianas. These systems significantly raise the cost and risk of U.S. and partner political, economic, and military activities.[175] Thus, even when operationally ready again, land force maneuver from the air or sea would by necessity be peripheral to avoid the greater risk inherent in it while accountable to a casualty-adverse American public. However, peripheral does not mean inconsequential. Combat maneuver missions that U.S. landpower can perform include the rapid protection of critical infrastructure (ports or pipelines) or choke points (against A2AD weapons by nonstate actors, for example), retaking disputed islands, raids, and halting destabilizing pirate activity (by seizing their havens) especially when these missions use surprise and are of limited scope.[176] Like maneuver, air and sea movement by land forces are important during contingency and humanitarian responses in which their mobility, light footprint, and logistics capabilities offer relief from natural disasters (like the seabasing response to the 2005 Indian Ocean tsunami disaster where some local ports were wiped out); man-made catastrophes (like the Fukushima Daiichi disaster in 2011); or to perform noncombatant rescue evacuations.[177] The threat environment in the

South China Sea could make combat use of landpower maneuver costly, but necessary, to give options to a joint force commander and dilemmas to an adversary. The difficulty in forcibly inserting and maneuvering land forces in the South China Sea dictates their cautious use, and the United States should instead consider substituting concentrated fires into the heart of A2AD areas as envisioned in the Air-Sea Battle concept.[178]

The first of the strategic roles of landpower, to compel or fight and win, dominantly influences and is influenced by the other strategic roles, as will be seen in the next sections on deterrence, and shaping and engaging. Landpower's contributions to these roles, through its inherent capabilities, are greater than is normally credited in a maritime environment. The U.S. Army's major role enabling other forces and agencies through its theater opening and sustaining abilities as the lead military service in logistics, mass transportation, communications, medical, and other support is very important. Through the core competency of wide area security, the U.S. Army with the Marine Corps is usually responsible for both passively and actively protecting forces, populations, and infrastructure against external and internal threats. The Army's air and missile defense systems are particularly needed in this A2AD environment against preemptive strikes, although their relatively short range and limited number currently make them defensive weapon systems. Another security role that land forces could play is sea-control from the land through anti-ship missiles, but no such capability currently exists and would require major acquisitions and force structure changes. However, this would be an important landpower contribution in a semi-enclosed maritime environment and one for which bipartisan support exists in the U.S. Congress. Although more offensive in nature, the counterland mission through surface-to-surface missiles also acts as a shield to suppress close-in attack systems based around the region and matches the escalation of Chinese missile deployments. A second core competency shared by the Marine Corps and Army is combined arms maneuver to achieve a relative position of advantage over an enemy. Amphibious operations, a mission assigned to all landpower forces, use the seabasing concept as a useful option during disasters and in the periphery, but are vulnerable in a dense A2AD environment. Maneuver by air offers another option, but is also vulnerable in the current environment. However, landpower's combat capabilities in the South China Sea may be most important, not in combat, but in its deterrence value and contributions to preventing war.

Landpower's Deter and Prevent Capabilities.

A major component of deterring and preventing conflict is the perceived ability to conduct combat operations credibly, such that aggressive outcomes by an adversary are stymied. If a state does not see the cost-benefit in its efforts, it will avoid conflict as detrimental to its interests.[179] Thus, U.S. landpower's capability to compel and fight, as presented in the previous section, is also critical to deterrence and prevention "by demonstrating the capability and resolve to apply force in pursuit of U.S. interests."[180] Plausible U.S. deterrence is underpinned by landpower to effectively communicate assurances of strong partnerships, a credible military presence, and an ability to deploy forces despite the A2AD threat.[181] U.S. deterrence ensures security through strengthening regional governments' legitimacy, promoting stability and prosperous economies, and encouraging vigorous foreign and military policy based on international rules in order to keep partner governments from being overwhelmed.[182] To make deterrence credible, U.S. land forces need to maintain a sufficient forward presence of forces, adequate prepositioning of equipment to support reinforcements, and effective crisis and contingency response operations, which are the major topics addressed in this section. West Point professor Robert Chamberlain believes "landpower is the only avenue by which America can enhance regional security and stability, deter Chinese militarism and encourage Chinese commitment to the global status quo" simultaneously.[183] In the coercive gradualism disputes common in the South China Sea, USARPAC strategy states that the ability to prevent war is as important as the ability to win a war.[184]

There is no better way to signal commitment, influence populations, and improve capabilities of other military forces than to have U.S. land forces interacting regularly with regional states as a stabilizing presence.[185] For example, the forward presence of land forces strengthens military deterrence by offering more opportunity for direct interaction to improve host nation military capabilities and interoperability with U.S. forces—significant enabling factors developed through interpersonal relations, security cooperation, and engagement, as shown later in this monograph.[186] Access to host nation bases better leverages the use of U.S. landpower, while partners and allies who cannot match American capabilities contribute tangibly to the partnership through sharing their facilities and territory.[187] U.S. land-based forces in the region also strengthen deterrence by reassuring partners and allies through sharing their vulnerability, dispersing and entwining forces among more installations to complicate an attack, and acting as a tripwire for a U.S. response, the ultimate guarantee of security for partners and U.S. interests.[188] Hosting U.S. forces may also result in improved or upgraded local combined-use infrastructure and better logistical support to host forces for equipment and services, especially those of U.S. origin.[189] Because of long lines of communication to Southeast Asia from the United States, forward presence forces negate the deployment time and vulnerability-in-transit of forces already in place, which can then better receive reinforcements and supplies.[190] From such considerations the *Joint Operational Access Concept* (JOAC) concludes, "The more capability and capacity that a military can amass at the forward base, the more it can mitigate the effects of distance."[191] U.S. policy emphasizes that such a presence is attained through rotating forces in Southeast Asia, where the United States has not had permanent bases or standing forces in decades. Thus, the plausibility of U.S. military deterrence is premised upon sufficient forward forces whose presence results in: capable, self-assured partners with whom trusted relationships are developed; collective interests that share defense costs and build interoperability; and a more dispersed and sustainable response to crises and contingencies.[192]

As part of the rebalance to Asia strategy, the 2014 QDR makes clear that the U.S. military presence in Southeast Asia needs to increase, and indications are that allies and partners would welcome such a move—on their terms.[193] If U.S. landpower is to exert its strengths and capabilities, it needs forward locations in order to protect, project power, and engage with regional forces when called upon. Hosting U.S.

forces entails one of three options: a few permanent, regularly-manned, hardened installations that can withstand attack but may be politically controversial and expensive to maintain; disperse rotational forces into more, but less-capable intermediate bases, which spread vulnerability but are more burdensome to protect and resupply; or temporary use of host-nation bases, although these facilities tend to be the most challenging for conducting operations and engagement as they are often austere and unfamiliar.[194] An example of permanent, hardened basing is the U.S. island territory of Guam, where foreign sovereignty issues are not a hindrance. In addition to having attack submarine and bomber bases, with fighters, aerial tankers, and remotely piloted vehicles (PRVs) coming in the near future, Marine and SOF numbers are building on Guam, which will make it the regional hub for amphibious and special operations.[195] Protective aircraft shelters, redundant pipelines, shielded land communications, and advanced logistics represent some of the hardenings that make Guam a formidable, but also an enticing target. For this reason, a U.S. Army THAAD battery is already stationed there, and other elements of landpower's wide area security should supplement that.[196] Dispersing forces to more numerous, but less improved, intermediate locations are best represented by the agreement to host 2,500 U.S. Marines with helicopters and aircraft in Darwin, Australia, on a steady rotational basis meant to improve training, interoperability, proximity to the region, and to disperse forces further.[197] Although both of these force-hosting-options indirectly support U.S. policy in Southeast Asia as described above, neither option is feasible for directly hosting U.S. forces in the region.

A third basing option, temporarily deploying forces to host-nation bases for limited periods (sometimes referred to as "lily-pads"), allows U.S. troops to train other forces, participate in exercises, or quickly reinforce a partner. Using more numerous and less-improved facilities on an occasional basis makes them less inviting targets and offers flexibility to commanders. However, unless using regionally aligned units recurrently, the force-to-force exchange advantage is markedly diminished at temporary facilities, and training, exercising, or operating from such sites is more difficult.[198] A good example of this option around the South China Sea littoral is the 2014 Enhanced Defense Cooperation Agreement (EDCA) with the Philippines, in which U.S. forces have regular access to five Armed Forces of the Philippines (AFP) facilities using rotating forces.[199] These facilities offer more advantageous proximity to the South China Sea, their number gives strategic depth, targeting them becomes riskier, and they convey commitment while less adversarial to China as temporary-use facilities.[200] However, the limited number of missile defense systems means some facilities could go unprotected when pressed into service or that forces become concentrated onto less hardened facilities. Such bases are also more vulnerable to the vagaries of diplomatic relations, as comments by President Duterte have made clear about withholding use of Filipino bases to U.S. forces. Of the bases offered, only one is a Philippine Army post, Fort Magsaysay, a key training area more useful for security cooperation activities than direct defense of the Philippines. The rest are air bases, which, if levied into U.S. use, would need missile and ground security provided by U.S. landpower. Other examples of this temporary option are deployed land forces for annual exercises to Vietnam or Malaysia, as explored further in the next section. Hardened, dispersed, or temporary forward basing by U.S. forces could reassure partners, deter aggression in peacetime, and give positional advantages to U.S. forces in an A2AD environment.[201]

A necessary auxiliary to forward presence is the prepositioning of equipment and supplies in forward locations where forces arriving by air transport can quickly set up operations using locally stored gear.[202] Prepositioning includes conventional combat, special operations, and port opening materials to defend allies and partners or engage with them though exercises and training.[203] Prepositioning is a form of forward presence with far fewer personnel, and thus may be more domestically acceptable for some countries and less likely to alienate host states from China.[204] Prepositioning reduces the A2AD in-transit risk and response time of deploying U.S. forces during a crisis, if properly pre-located, and cuts transportation costs for recurring exercises or training.[205] In response to Chinese militarization of the South China Sea, the U.S. Army may respond by prepositioning additional or upgraded unit combat equipment or by establishing War Reserve Stocks for Allies to directly support a partner in the region.[206] However, there are fiscal costs under a constricted budget, from purchasing additional needed material to stock the reserves, to maintaining and upgrading equipment to keep it operationally ready.[207]

In 2016, the U.S. Army began to preposition material in the region through the Army Prepositioned Stocks (APS) Program, starting with activity sets for Humanitarian Assistance and Disaster Response (HA/DR) covering tasks such as engineering, medical care, or civil affairs.[208] Prepositioning HA/DR sets, under DoD's Overseas Humanitarian, Disaster, and Civic Aid program, should be less controversial to all regional states and would likely be used in a permissive environment in which stocks may be easily moved around the region with intra-theater lift.[209] Under the Philippines EDCA, port opening, HA/DR, and engagement activity sets may be prepositioned to serve a variety of missions, although President Duterte's suspicions of these sites may hamper their use while he remains in power.[210] In 2016, Cambodia agreed to host U.S. Army prepositioned HA/DR reserves including de-mining, engineering, and port opening equipment, as have Vietnam and Malaysia. The Army is looking to expand this program throughout the Pacific region.[211] China will likely disapprove of prepositioned equipment, especially in countries that had not closely cooperated before with U.S. land forces, and thus could fuel a sense of encirclement by China.[212] Such a depot may then also become a lucrative preemptive target.[213] In addition to its land-stored prepositioned equipment, the Army also has two reserves aboard ships to give its stores more flexibility and less predictability.[214] Through the Maritime Prepositioning Force Operations, prepositioning of gear aboard ships is the Marine Corps' primary reserves in the region using the 3rd Maritime Prepositioning Ship Squadron, based in Guam, to resupply a Marine EF of up to 18,000 marines for 30 days of operations, ranging from combat to humanitarian assistance.[215] Prepositioning of equipment reduces costs, improves response time, opens opportunities for further engagement, and forms the base for other aspects of deterrence such as U.S. landpower's ability to effectively respond to crises and limited contingencies in the South China Sea region, which are major missions of the U.S. Army and Marine Corps.[216]

However, access agreements, capable forces, and prepositioned material are only part of deterrence. The demonstrated will to use military force is another critical aspect that in part is manifested through support to partner and ally states during a crisis or contingency. According to Marine Corps doctrine:

Crisis response and limited contingency operations encompass a variety of military actions, often in support of other government agencies, to contain or mitigate the effects of natural disasters or calamitous human events . . . requiring a military response regardless of ongoing operations elsewhere."[217]

The onset of an emergent situation and its importance to national interests distinguishes between a crisis and contingency, but the commitment to maintaining functionality, stability, and legitimacy in cooperating countries is what makes both types of responses important for deterrence.[218] Countering insurgencies, terrorism, or violent criminal trafficking are examples of U.S. landpower's welcomed involvement in internal security and stability responses that enhance deterrence.[219] U.S. landpower can also oppose opportunistic external aggression through fulfilling security agreements like the *Mutual Defense Treaty between the Philippines and the United States*, and demonstrate support for friendly governments when confronting coercive gradualism if invoked.[220] Land forces, with other elements of national power, effectively support deterrence and stability to enable domestic forces to better support their governments.[221] Because of its specialized functions, SOF has not played a major role in the landpower missions presented so far, but during crises and limited contingencies, SOF involvement can be significant.[222] For example, Joint Special

Operations Task Force—Philippines (JSOTF-P) was a primarily SOF-led mission that worked and collocated with AFP forces against dangerous extremists intent on disrupting Philippine governance in its southern islands. From 2002 to 2014, U.S. SOF helped to counter the Abu Sayyaf and Jemaah Islamiyah groups through advising during AFP operations, training Philippine forces, and rendering humanitarian assistance and medical projects to improve conditions for indigenous people.[223] Concerns are rising that Southeast Asia may be in peril by a large number of extremists, who joined the Islamic State of Iraq and Syria (ISIS) in the Middle East, returning to Malaysia, Indonesia, and the Philippines to form a new core for terrorism and insurgency that may again require the expertise of U.S. landpower to stem, although the Duterte administration now seems antithetical to more U.S. counterinsurgency support.[224] U.S. landpower's crucial support to allies and partners during security responses, best demonstrated by JSOTF-P, enhance regional states' legitimacy and stability by stopping internal problems that divert attention from international challenges or by preventing international aggression from spawning internal problems, and thus reinforces internal stability and legitimacy to prevent war.

In addition to countering internal and external political challenges, U.S. landpower is a key player in mitigating the natural and man-made catastrophes that could upset stability within regional states.[225] The South China Sea borders the geologically active Pacific Ring of Fire and is the main thoroughfare of Typhoon Alley, and thus is susceptible to natural disasters "worsened by a lack of disaster mitigation [in] city planning . . . [and] social infrastructure, and HA/DR [humanitarian assistance and disaster response] capabilities in regional armed forces. Poor disaster management has the potential to trigger political and economic unrest."[226] Humanitarian and disaster responses often rely on landpower capabilities to supplement relief agencies and host government efforts, while under the lead of another U.S. agency.[227] The key response roles of foreign humanitarian assistance (FHA) and consequence management (CM) complement one another in that FHA relieves or reduces "the results of natural or man-made disasters . . . [and] is generally limited in scope and duration," while CM are "actions taken to maintain or restore essential services and manage and mitigate problems resulting from disasters and catastrophes, including natural, man-made, or terrorist incidents."[228]

U.S. landpower is needed especially in these roles with other agencies: for its rapid response, while working in non-permissive or austere conditions, when access is difficult, and after local agencies are overwhelmed or exhausted. Particularly valued in accomplishing these tasks are the SOFs "geographic orientation, cultural knowledge, language capabilities, and the ability to work with multiethnic indigenous populations and international relief organizations to provide initial and ongoing assessments. . . . [SOF civil affairs units] are particularly well-suited for stabilization efforts in disaster areas" because they have the expertise to best liaison with civil organizations, and can integrate and direct essential military functions.[229] To mitigate disasters, conventional Army and Marine Corps forces enable security, logistics, engineering, transport, medical, and command and communications support to restore infrastructure and protect and sustain victims.[230] An example of landpower acting in FHA was in November 2013, when nearly 1,000 U.S.

marines and their aircraft, supported by U.S. Navy assets, responded to the devastation of the central Philippines by Super Typhoon Haiyan, the strongest typhoon ever recorded. With USAID as the lead U.S. agency, and while coordinating closely with the AFP, JTF 505 cleared roads and opened airports, provided vital communications support, conducted search and rescue operations, gave medical care, transported aid workers, distributed 2,495 tons of relief supplies, and evacuated 21,000 people—thereby ameliorating a humanitarian disaster.[231] Other recent examples of U.S. land forces significantly supporting relief operations include the 2011 seismic and nuclear disaster in central Japan, the 2015 response to Typhoon Soudelor in the Northern Marianas and the earthquakes in Nepal, and the 2016 earthquake in southern Japan.[232] Elements of deterrence, such as regular cooperation and forward basing, enhance crisis and contingency responses to security and humanitarian issues, but response operations also bolster deterrence and support closer ties and mutual interests like respect for human values.[233]

The second of the strategic roles of U.S. landpower—deter and prevent war—is crucial to stability in Southeast Asia and reinforces landpower's other strategic roles. Credible deterrence that thwarts an adversary's aggressive intentions requires the operational capabilities that U.S. landpower offers, as covered in the combat and compel section of this monograph. However, deterrence also needs to exhibit the will to back those capabilities that are demonstrated through the forward presence of troops and prepositioning of equipment, thus making plausible U.S. intentions in the South China Sea region. The advantage of forward positioned troops can be gained through hardened, dispersed, or temporary facilities that result in reduced cost and risk with increased speed of deployments, and improved support and engagement of allies and partners. U.S. landpower's ability to help mitigate crises and contingencies, whether security related or natural or man-made disasters, "employ[s] military capabilities alongside partners with very little to no strategic warning, in effect serving as a useful demonstration of latent U.S. contingency response capability," as shown by JSOTF-P and JTF 505 in the Philippines.[234] U.S. landpower's presence in the region also has a stabilizing effect by being a committed but defensive signal of American interests in support of partners, humanitarian values, and international norms in much the same way U.S. Forces Korea's landpower has for over 60 years. This is because of the resolve that land forces represent when committed by the U.S. Government, and the powerful influence landpower wields in the human domain "largely because it puts U.S. forces in direct contact with those they seek to influence; whether by deterring or halting enemies, or by convincing civilian policymakers and populations that they share objectives and priorities with the United States."[235] With forward presence and operationally interacting with the forces of Southeast Asia, U.S. forces have more opportunity to assure partners while improving host nation military capabilities and interoperability through the shaping and engagement actions of security cooperation, which are presented next.

Landpower's Engage and Shape Capabilities.

The third strategic role of U.S. landpower—to engage states and shape conditions—may be the most important because it sets the foundation for U.S. and regional forces to win or prevent conflict.[236] Shaping is the establishment of conditions in which U.S. and partners' interests may be met by favorably influencing the operational area and the human domain.[237] These conducive future conditions are attained during operational planning's Phase Zero through a variety of peacetime security cooperation, engagement, and bilateral and multinational activities.[238] Shaping operations squarely align with a third of the U.S. Army's missions, to "provide a global stabilizing presence," and more specifically with its proposed core capability to "shape the security environment."[239] Military engagement is the art of shaping human activities through interactions between U.S. and other countries' forces "designed to build trust and confidence, share information, coordinate mutual activities, and maintain influence" in order to better understand and affect the security and human environments.[240] "Engage and partner" is a critical line of effort for USARPAC's "operations, actions, and activities to assure security and stability." Similarly, U.S. Marine Corps doctrine states that military engagement and security cooperation "build partnerships that promote a collective approach to mutual security concerns," and in joint doctrine for SOF it serves to reduce daily tensions, collect information to forewarn of crisis, and "develop and build [host nation] capabilities and capacities that can be leveraged in crises and war."[241] A more specific form of engagement with respect to China is also used in this monograph as the "means to improve the non-status quo elements of a rising major power's behavior . . . [to] induce a rising power to adopt foreign or domestic policies in line with the norms of the dominant international order."[242] With the U.S. State Department as the lead agency for foreign policy, these are tasks in which landpower excels because of the human-to-human contact with the powerful land forces in the region, but which play a mainly protective, non-threatening role around the South China Sea.[243] The rest of this monograph explains how engagement and shaping address U.S. interests through capacity building and security cooperation with allies, partners, and other countries in the region.[244]

Shaping and engagement are important to U.S. and partner interests because they create a favorable environment and future in which to operate. U.S. landpower is a major tool in creating that environment through building partner capacity (BPC), described by former U.S. Secretary of Defense Robert Gates as "helping other countries defend themselves or, if necessary, fight alongside U.S. forces by providing them with equipment, training, or other forms of security assistance."[245] The intent of BPC is to help partners meet basic defense needs and build self-confidence in their security capabilities in order to contribute to regional security with the United States and other partners.[246] For the United States, BPC offers the advantages of sharing costs and responsibilities for local and collective security with other countries, exerting positive U.S. leadership in attaining mutual interests, and bolstering defense credibility through multilateral and regional ties—and doing so cost-effectively.[247] For U.S. landpower in particular, BPC improves military preparedness and interoperability with partners, spreads "burden-sharing and harnesses economies of scale based on common systems," may cover regional shortfalls in U.S. capabilities and capacity, and "shortens friendly response times and increases uncertainty for an adversary."[248] U.S. landpower's BPC has recently developed counterterrorism, counterinsurgency, and disaster assistance skills with the many countries sharing an interest in the South China Sea region, but it also develops full spectrum partner capabilities against A2AD threats in areas that U.S. land-power has the expertise to share.[249] DoD's $425 million Southeast Asia Reassurance Fund is a BPC initiative meant mainly to improve at-sea capabilities for partners, but it could also enhance landpower's fires and maneuver at sea by investing in the maritime domain awareness initiative from which air, sea, and land forces synergistically benefit, especially if enhancing nascent collective security efforts coordinated with regional leaders like Australia and Japan.[250] BPC is an important element of statecraft and security in Southeast Asia, and U.S. landpower plays a major role in its effectiveness.

A multiplying factor in BPC (and for combat and deterrence missions) is the interpersonal and organizational relations in which U.S. landpower excels. The expertise in regional and cultural matters leveraged by SOF, regionally aligned conventional land forces, forward presence units, and specialist foreign area officers builds stronger partnerships and engages friends and competitors in enduring relationships that make other efforts more effective—especially in disaster response and foreign internal defense.[251] These contacts potentially benefit both partners through improved capabilities and assurances of U.S. support, but they also enable a "land network of relationships resulting in early warning, indigenous solutions . . . informed campaigns," shared intelligence, realistic training, and increased cultural awareness that benefit overall U.S. interests as well.[252] Shaping and influencing other populations is a difficult, inexact art that can be counterproductive if done poorly; but fruitful interactions are invaluable if at least for the better understanding of the other's fundamental objectives that may identify areas of mutual interest.[253] If done well, BPC can progress to the point where the United States does not need to be the regional initiator of such efforts, but instead like-minded states train and exercise together, reinforcing intra-regional ties and building credible collective security.[254] U.S. landpower is attractive to regional military forces because of its flexible array of much-needed combat and combat support capabilities (as detailed in the combat and compel section) delivered through BPC by experts in military and civilian fields—the latter in the form of reserve component soldiers and marines offering excellent insight into civil-military relations.[255] These very influential land-force-to-land-force ties within Southeast Asia also benefit U.S. air and sea forces and other government agencies through greater partner confidence in the United States and improved access to partners.[256] An example is the improving of U.S. military ties with Vietnam to help integrate that country into the current international order, which opens doors to address security issues of mutual concern.[257] U.S. landpower's abilities to assure and engage in the human domain are a boon to the United States, its regional partners, and other states.

The formal term for the many security interactions described in this monograph is security cooperation, defined as DoD:

> interactions with foreign defense establishments to build defense relationships that promote specific US security interests, develop allied and friendly military capabilities for self-defense and multinational operations, and provide US forces with peacetime and contingency access to a host nation.[258]

Security cooperation, also previously known as military-to-military activities, is a key element of shaping and engaging operations at the strategic level and is usually conducted under the funding and oversight of the State Department as a part of U.S. foreign policy.[259] It seeks to improve access to, and the military capability of, partner forces and their interoperability with U.S. and other friendly forces. In addition, for more advanced allies like Australia and Japan, security cooperation strives to assist in their regional leadership roles of protecting security and stability.[260] With emerging or rival powers like China, security cooperation also works to deepen relationships to increase mutual understanding, reduce tensions, and to pursue common objectives found in areas like humanitarian assistance and peacekeeping operations.[261] USPACOM organizes these shaping and engagement activities through its Theater Security Cooperation Plan (TSCP), in conjunction with each American embassy's country plan, delegating activities to its service sub-components like USARPAC, MARFORPAC, and SOCPAC as part of their "day-to-day mission of . . . 'fighting phase zero'."[262] U.S. landpower's role in security cooperation is particularly potent because all states in the region have a corresponding land force that tends to be the senior service in terms of domestic influence, and because U.S. land forces like SOF and regionally aligned conventional forces have developed expertise in training and long-term relations with their counterparts, which leverages their influence significantly.[263] Throughout the Pacific region, for example, USARPAC has conducted over 200 major bilateral and multilateral TSCP events annually, including 26 major exercises, humanitarian responses and training, key leader engagements, advise and equip foreign forces, peace operations training, personnel exchanges, reconstruction, conferences, information and intelligence sharing, military education, and many other activities—with examples from the South China Sea region presented below.[264] Each of these security cooperation activities is meant to improve self-defense, interoperability, and access in order to attain U.S. and partner goals for regional security and stability.

Security cooperation is a wide-ranging collection of U.S. military activities with regional forces. A part of it is security assistance, which is the provision of "defense articles, military training, and other defense-related services by grant, loan, credit, or cash sales in furtherance of national policies and objectives," as overseen by the State Department.[265] Although needed arms, equipment, defense services, and schoolhouse training may be directly purchased commercially by other countries, in Southeast Asia defense articles are usually obtained through the U.S. Government's foreign military sales (FMS) program. This program reinforces the advantages of engagement cited throughout this monograph to include bolstering each country's self-defense and interoperability with partners, reducing the cost of common systems, and establishing enduring relationships and influence.[266] The U.S. Army Security Assistance Command (USASAC), for instance, provides, sustains, and trains on Army articles used by other countries, for which the Pacific region has been a major customer, especially for items such as helicopters and missile systems.[267] Formal education and training are also part of FMS, in which international students may attend U.S. military schools, or U.S. teams train individuals and units at their home stations using programs like International Military Education and Training (IMET) administered by the military services' security assistance agencies. An example would be the Philippine, Malaysian, and Vietnamese officers who attend the U.S. Army War College (USAWC) annually or others who attend technical training in the United States for a specific weapon system.[268]

Outside of security assistance, security cooperation takes such forms as exercises and military-to-military engagement in the South China Sea region. Combined exercises are effective tools for training with single and multiple partner states, and for improving interoperability while familiarizing U.S. forces with local conditions and personnel. Within the region, exercises leveraging recent U.S. land force experiences "that focus on counter-terror, humanitarian assistance, disaster relief, pandemic response, transnational crime, and peacekeeping operations" are in demand and will likely increase.[269] One important exercise program is USARPAC's Pacific Pathways, meant to improve multilateral interoperability and develop networks of trust and understanding through three annual deployments meant to expand the Army's role in the region by projecting tailored and ready forces to participate in sequential exercises for 3- to 4-month deployments that optimize the cost of training, allow U.S. forces to bring more and heavier equipment resulting in more robust engagement, and offers flexibility in establishing a forward U.S. presence and improving interoperability. For example, in the 2016 Pacific Pathways, the U.S. 2nd Stryker Brigade participated in sequential bilateral exercises in Thailand, Indonesia, and Malaysia with armored vehicles while monitored from a forward command post set up at Fort Magsaysay in the Philippines.[270] Another example is one of the U.S. military's largest exercises, the annual Cobra Gold held in Thailand, with more than 30 countries participating, including Malaysia and Indonesia (or observing, like Vietnam), in a series of activities ranging from live-fire combined arms combat maneuvers, to disaster relief or humanitarian mission command post exercises.[271] The world's largest multilateral maritime exercise, Rim of the Pacific (RIMPAC) is held in and around Hawaii and includes land forces participating in realistic amphibious operations that were led by a New Zealand Navy Commodore in 2016. The more than 25,000 participants from 27 countries include members from Brunei, Indonesia, Malaysia, the Philippines, and China to a limited degree, and the diversity is meant to sustain cooperative relationships.[272] Forward deployed marines in Australia will extensively train with their counterparts at local training ranges, and from there and from Okinawa, deploy on shorter duration training exercises in the region, especially amphibious operations and HA/DR missions for which there is increasing demand for Marine Corps expertise. Improved interoperability could lead to a "regional 'amphibious architecture' composed of cooperative nations with capabilities that make them better able to defend themselves and be more useful partners," both tactically and strategically.[273]

Shaping and engaging are also performed through military-to-military relationships from the individual to the unit level. The formal education and exercise opportunities already cited are examples of building such relationships. Other examples are the senior officer level dialogues, expert exchanges, and staff assistance visits that allow frank discussions on issues that cross borders such as infectious diseases and military medicine, transnational crime, and natural disasters.[274] USARPAC regularly hosts the Pacific Armies

Chiefs Conference and the Pacific Armies Management Seminar (PAMS) for senior level officers from across the Asia-Pacific region to engage one another to "foster better understandings of the dynamic and complex issues that affect all nations throughout the region."[275] Similarly, MARFORPAC initiated the Pacific Command Amphibious Leaders Symposium (PALS) in 2015 to include officers from 22 countries including Malaysia, the Philippines, Vietnam, Indonesia, Australia, and Japan "to discuss each nation's goals while working with one another to strengthen bilateral and multilateral relationships through future engagements and training," especially in HA/DR and collective maritime domain awareness.[276] Military exchanges with officers serving temporarily in the service of another country are also useful immersions in understanding and interoperability, with Australian Major General Richard Burr, for example, seconded as the USARPAC Deputy Commanding General for Operations from 2013 to 2015.[277] U.S. marines serve on military staffs in Japan, Australia, and New Zealand to improve amphibious capabilities, following the model of the successful transformation of South Korea's marines after years of association with their U.S. counterparts.[278] The U.S. Army's Regionally Aligned Forces (RAF), from Washington State's I Corps to Hawaii's 25th Infantry Division, brigade combat teams, and Pacific Rim National Guard units, are assigned to engage solely with Asia-Pacific states to:[279]

> not only learn the specifics of a particular locality but also gain a broader ability to rapidly develop situational understanding in the event of a contingency operation anywhere. They are expert in their combat skills, and when coupled with U.S.-based global response forces, these regionally aligned forces [RAF] provide

> a powerful blend of local knowledge and large-scale capabilities that can execute the full spectrum of activities from security cooperation to support to counterterrorism to large-scale contingency response. . . . The U.S. Army, along with special operations forces and the U.S. Marine Corps, form the core of a global landpower network.[280]

U.S. landpower's ability to shape and engage results in:

> interactions with foreign defense establishments to build defense relationships that promote specific US security interests, develop allied and friendly military capabilities for self-defense and multinational operations, and provide US forces with peacetime and contingency access to a host nation.[281]

This is accomplished through BPC, military-to-military engagements, and security cooperation, at which landpower excels. These strengths are best exemplified in the specific activities presented below involving Vietnam, Malaysia, the Philippines, and China.

Conflict with China and subsequent tensions in the South China Sea have spurred Vietnam to improve relations with the United States since the Vietnam War.[282] "Vietnam is the most capable and determined Southeast Asian state to challenge China's claims in the South China Sea" and the most active in multilateral efforts to counter aggression.[283] That provides sufficient mutual national interests for U.S. landpower to meaningfully engage with Vietnam. USARPAC categorizes its engagement efforts at one of five levels (see Figure 2), and Vietnam might be placed in the middle "enhance critical capabilities" class defined as:

countries that have expressed a desire for a closer comprehensive security partnership with the United States but lack the military resiliency and capacity to exert significant military influence beyond their immediate borders. In many cases, these countries acknowledge the stabilizing influence of America's regional presence; however, direct or long-term employment of U.S. forces could be objectionable, infeasible, or counterproductive. USARPAC seeks opportunities to improve relationships by *enhancing* specific capabilities, such as peacekeeping, humanitarian assistance, or disaster relief [italics in original].[284]

The military relationship with Vietnam is based on a limited defense cooperation agreement signed in September 2011 and enhanced in July 2015 to an "extensive comprehensive partnership" to guide future military cooperation between the two.[285] Nonetheless, Vietnam has even closer strategic ties with India, Japan, and Russia, with the latter supplying nearly all of Vietnam's weapons, in a delicate diplomatic balance in which China is prominent.[286] To continue to build relations, American and Vietnamese land forces have engaged in high-level dialogues, humanitarian assistance agreements, combined search and rescue and disaster relief exercises, military training and education, sharing of counterterrorism intelligence, and peacekeeping training.[287] Such contacts flourish despite Vietnam's sub-standard human rights record because these activities enhance the humanitarian nature and promise of influence in improving civil-military relations and respect for civil rights.[288]

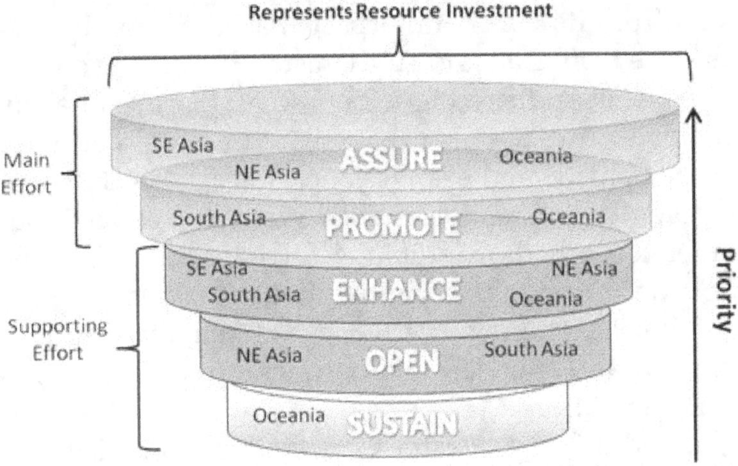

**Figure 2. USARPAC Theater Engagement
and Partner Design.**[289]

Vietnam has identified illicit trafficking, transnational crimes, and illegal immigration as other areas of concern in which U.S. landpower may fruitfully engage.[290] For instance, since 2012, the Oregon National Guard has been linked with the Vietnamese People's Army (VPA) through the State Partnership Program (SPP). The distinctive state-federal and civil-military characteristics of the national guard, and its experience in civil emergencies, border protection, natural and man-made disaster preparedness, and combat skills mutually builds both sides' capabilities, cross-cultural awareness, and international relationship through long-term interaction.[291] Peacekeeping operations are another area of mutual interest, and the U.S. Army's Peacekeeping and Stability Operations Institute (PKSOI) assisted Vietnam to establish the Vietnam Peacekeeping Center in 2015 and 2016. The VPA is also interested in learning advanced field medical skills from its U.S. counterparts based on combat experience from Iraq and Afghanistan.[292] Some exercises have been conducted too, including an army-to-army combined exercise in urban search and rescue with more sophisticated exercises possible.[293] Another area of potential interaction is with Vietnam's capable but under-resourced amphibious forces with which the U.S. Marines could be influential through the PALS regional amphibious network, yet remain HA/DR-oriented and thus less likely to irritate Chinese-Vietnamese relations.[294]

In addition to exercises, training, and visits by American personnel, a forward presence by U.S. land forces was negotiated in 2016 with Vietnam hosting U.S. Army prepositioned HA/DR reserves, including a field hospital.[295] The United States would like to expand its presence at Cam Ranh Bay, one of the best natural harbors in the region and a major logistical and intermodal hub for the United States during its war in Vietnam.[296] Facilities there currently repair U.S. commercial and non-combat military logistics vessels, and expanding access could eventually require U.S. landpower's wide area defense and port and logistics services to maintain a major entry point into Indochina, and a facility from which to pursue security cooperation further. However, Vietnamese officials prefer a non-committed use of its facilities, catering instead to all of its strategic partners.[297] Another aspect of improving relations is through FMS. In 2014, the United States relaxed the ban on selling non-lethal military equipment to Vietnam; and, in 2016, during a visit to Vietnam, former President Obama opened sales for all military equipment on a case-by-case basis in order to counter aggressive Chinese moves in the South China Sea.[298] Full access to U.S. arms has long been a goal of Vietnam to show that relations with the United States have been normalized and to improve its A2AD naval and coastal defenses.[299] U.S. landpower could assist with some items needed by Vietnam, including artillery and missile systems; command, control, communications, and intelligence systems; helicopters; amphibious craft; and spare parts for equipment left by the United States in 1975.[300] U.S. land forces could also be instrumental with the PVA-dominated military in implementing a regional maritime domain awareness initiative as it develops.[301] U.S. landpower's engagement with Vietnam is vital to enhance this military partner's civil and defense capabilities to meet common aspirations through training activities, visits, dialogues, and prepositioning and sales of military equipment that are part of greater shape and engage operations.

Unlike Vietnam, Malaysia has maintained a long cordial partnership with the United States. It also maintains excellent relationships with its Association of Southeast Asian Nations (ASEAN) neighbors and tries to balance good relations with China, but aggressive stances against Malaysian claims in the South China Sea and militarization of land features has resulted in Malaysia's Government hedging against Chinese actions.[302] The U.S. relationship with Malaysia may be encapsulated by USARPAC's engagement effort level of "promote regional leadership," defined as:

These countries have stated aspirations to expand their regional influence generally in common with U.S. interests and expressed their intentions and willingness to use their influence to assume a greater share of future regional security responsibilities. Their defense establishments demonstrate overall military resiliency and increased professionalism . . . the U.S. now seeks to *promote* key aspects of their military capacity to achieve their regional security aspirations [italics in original].[303]

Security cooperation between the United States and Malaysia is strengthening, as is U.S. cooperation with neighbors Indonesia and Brunei. The U.S.-Malaysian partnership is manifest in diverse activities such as exercises between each country's military services and multinational maneuvers like Cobra Gold; combined training especially in jungle warfare; exchange visits and port calls; use of some U.S. military equipment and a small amount of FMS funding; IMET with funding; and counter-piracy operations.[304] There is no SPP between the Malaysian military and U.S. National Guard forces yet, but Malaysian and Bruneian officials have shown some interest to follow Indonesia, which has partnered with the Hawaii National Guard since 2006.[305] The United States strives to sustain its friendly, relatively sophisticated relationship with Malaysia through engagement in meeting their common goals for security and stability in the region.

Although the Malaysian Army is the senior service in the Malaysian Armed Forces, most of Malaysia's external threats (pirates, illegal immigration, Sulu insurgents, and Chinese encroachment on Malaysian South China Sea claims) are seaborne. The Malaysian Army is addressing these by transforming one of its paratrooper brigades into a new amphibious unit based on the U.S. Marine Corps.[306] The resulting interaction since 2014 is a model for landpower engagement. U.S. Marine Corps training assistance started with the Malaysia-United States Amphibious Exercise 2015 in North Borneo, consisting of training, planning, and execution of combined amphibious air-ground operations; a live-fire demonstration; and weapons familiarization. In turn, jungle-fighting training was led by Malaysian soldiers, and cultural exchanges of sports competitions were included.[307] The Malaysian Defense Minister Hishammuddin Hussein stated such exercises could "pave the way for future exercises in Malaysia" and proposed that ASEAN "create a ready group that focuses on humanitarian assistance and disaster response capabilities."[308] Another exercise, Keris Strike, is an annual army-to-army engagement hosted in Malaysia since 1996 to improve military readiness and tactical interoperability. In 2015, key events were a command post exercise; jungle field training; training in unmanned aerial surveillance, medical response, counter-improvised explosive devices; and an engineer civil action project. Keris Strike was also one of the exercises included in the 2014 Pacific Pathways.[309]

Two other aspects of security cooperation with Malaysia are forward presence and sales of military equipment. The recurring training visits, exercises, aircraft servicing, and an increasing number of naval vessel port calls in Malaysia are supported by the 1994 Acquisition and Cross Servicing Agreement, which also allows U.S. SOF to practice at the Malaysian Jungle Warfare Training School.[310] Malaysia has also agreed to store U.S. Army prepositioned engineering, water production, and transportation gear in the near future. The Malaysian Government has a policy of spreading military acquisitions among many sources, so U.S. equipment is only modestly represented in its ranks, but each of the Malaysian services uses the U.S. M4 carbine rifle. The Malaysian Army also needs helicopters to defend its South China Sea coastlines and is in negotiations for the Bell AH-1Z Super Cobra attack helicopter and MD 530G scout attack helicopter, and currently operates a few Sikorsky H-60 Blackhawk and S-61 Nuri utility helicopters.[311] Good long-term relations between the United States and Malaysia have sustained strong landpower engagement between the two in a variety of areas that benefit both countries' strategic interests.

Since becoming treaty allies in 1951, and with colonial ties dating to the 1890s, U.S.-Philippine relations have climbed and dipped, but in 2015 were at a zenith in large part because of mutual efforts to combat terrorism and Chinese maritime aggression, before reaching a nadir with President Duterte's ambivalence toward the United States.[312] Nonetheless, this long-standing treaty relationship with the Philippines is reflected in USARPAC's closest engagement level of "assure allies and partners," which are:

> relatively sophisticated and long-standing defense partnerships in which the U.S. seeks to *assure* partners of its mutual defense commitment . . . what sets this class of nations apart is a binding and durable commitment to take action together to counter shared threats. . . . Exercises and engagements seek to reinforce interoperability. . . . Based on the importance of these defense relationships . . . USARPAC Commander focuses the preponderance of resources, time, and effort to maintain strong partnerships with them. Significantly, USARPAC often partners with MARFORPAC and SOCPAC in building ground force capacity throughout the AOR, but particularly with these partners [italics in original].[313]

Since 1998, the two states have renewed a Status of Forces Agreement and, in 2002, established a Mutual Logistics Support Agreement, which allowed a robust schedule of exercises, military visits, and basing of operational activities such as JSOTF-P. The Philippines military benefited from about 400 planned annual activities with U.S. forces, an active IMET program, and the Excess Defense Articles Program (EDAP), which transfers surplus U.S. military equipment at low or no cost in order to modernize partner states.[314] After long neglect, the Philippine Government is modernizing AFP defense capabilities with significantly increased spending, and U.S. landpower can support some Philippine requirements for amphibious, wide area protection, and ocean and air surveillance and defense capabilities, when relations improve in the future perhaps under or after the Trump administration.[315] For instance, the new Philippine National Coastal Watch Center was built using a $20 million U.S. Government grant; intelligence sharing, maritime surveillance, and secure communications bolstered with $40 million; the Philippine Army received 100 excess M113 armored personnel carriers under the EDAP; and a new program has been started to improve the Philippine Army's air assault capabilities.[316] Just as important, U.S. land forces can assist in improving the inadequate Philippine supply and logistics, maintenance, and procurement processes at which the U.S. Army and Marine Corps excel.[317] Such continuing assurance to a treaty ally, despite recent turmoil in relations, underscores the U.S. defense commitment to the Philippines and gives legitimacy to the U.S. involvement in the South China Sea.[318]

Land forces' military-to-military relations between the United States and the Philippines has traditionally been strong, based upon working together operationally to counter terrorism, in response to disasters, and upon decades of training and exercising together. As both homeland defense and disaster relief remain major missions of the Philippine Army, U.S. land forces will continue their role in closely supporting them. The Philippine Army would also like to build its capacity to participate in peacekeeping operations in which the U.S. Army has the expertise to share.[319] Since 2000, the U.S. National Guard units in Hawaii and Guam and the Philippine military have also benefited from close ties through the SPP, which complements and enhances the many other activities regularly occurring between the two countries.[320] The Philippine and U.S. Marine Corps have long close ties with regular annual amphibious landing exercises that improved the skills and interoperability of both.[321] Major exercises include the biannual Balikatan, which, since 1984, focuses on humanitarian assistance and disaster relief capabilities and modernization. The 2016 exercise included approximately 5,000 U.S., 3,500 Philippine, and 80 Australian defense personnel engaged in HA/DR scenarios and civic assistance to local communities. It also added force integration training directed at maritime security and territorial defense, and the possibility of Japanese forces participating in the future.[322] A second long-running bilateral annual exercise, Philippine Amphibious Landing Exercise (PHIBLEX), focused more on combined arms amphibious training including raids, beach landings, and live fire exercises—which have recently been conducted near the Spratly Islands and Scarborough Shoal—while also improving interoperability for HA/DR crises. These 1- to 2-week exercises included a civic assistance component such as engineering projects to improve local infrastructure and health engagements.[323] The results of such efforts have been excellent military-to-military relations and effective disaster relief responses, which is why their current curtailment by the Duterte administration is a definite setback. Despite these efforts, combat capabilities, like amphibious assault operations, still need to be improved, because the Philippines was overly dependent upon the United States for its security, even while it periodically distances itself from its U.S. ally and leaves the United States in a difficult supporting position.[324]

One of the biggest contributions the Philippines makes to its U.S. partnership is offering a forward presence in close proximity to the South China Sea. The United States permanently stationed military forces in the Philippines for nearly a century until 1991, when they were removed at the Philippine Government's request. JSOTF-P reintroduced a U.S. presence after the September 11, 2001 attacks, with expanded rotational access for other U.S. forces allowed under the ECDA after 2014.[325] The subsequent Philippine Air Force bases approved for U.S. use are Antonio Bautista AB (on Palawan), Basa AB and Fort Magsaysay (on Luzon), Lumbia AB (on Mindanao), and Mactan-Benito Ebuen AB (on Cebu), with U.S. Marines rotating through the Philippine Marines headquarters at Camp Aguinaldo, and requests to also use the former U.S. bases at Subic Bay and Clark International Airport, both now major civilian commercial hubs.[326] These are temporary U.S.-use installations where U.S. forces may preposition equipment to enhance training, exercises, contingencies, and combat operations. U.S. forces may also upgrade approved existing facilities and military infrastructure for combined use at each location.[327] Although the use by U.S. forces is rotational, there were opportunities for longer-term forward presence in some cases. For instance, after the departure of the 5,000 U.S. service members participating in Balikatan 2016, 275 remained behind with some equipment at different locations, to be replaced by other personnel later.[328] Additional longer-term deployments may follow, with more U.S. land forces involved as their combat, contingency, and support skills grow in demand and the U.S.-Philippine relationship builds, although a more balanced approach in 2016 between China and the United States by the new administration of President Duterte may moderate this.[329] Should relations improve, regular forward presence could leverage the effects of all other U.S. engagement with the Philippines and other regional states, and significantly strengthen U.S. deterrence and combat positions by presenting more operating locations, faster response to a contingency or crises, and complicating an adversary's targeting plan—all to help assure a long-time U.S. ally.[330]

The most important engagement around the South China Sea is between China and the United States, because how these ties develop in large part determines the rest of the relationships in the region. Following the political oscillations from World War II allies to Cold War enemies, more recent military-to-military relations between China and the United States are affected by internal events like the Tiananmen Square protests, arms sales to and crises over Taiwan, or international freedom of navigation incidents sparked by events like the EP-3E Aries II aircraft collision and militarization of South China Sea features.[331] Based upon fluctuating historic ties and the conflicting signals from current events, analysts differ widely on whether a U.S. strategy with China should be confrontational by directly countering Chinese actions or indirectly through actions to enhance partners, contain Chinese aggression from afar, or engage with China to manage an internationally acceptable accommodation of its power. William "Trey" Braun, an Asia and landpower expert at the U.S. Army's Strategic Studies Institute (SSI), sees the United States pursuing a "cooperative competitive strategy" with China in economic and diplomatic affairs, but a "coercive/confrontational competitive strategy" on military and information lines, which challenges the American public and its leaders to understand the "interplay between cooperative and coercive activity to avoid unintended consequences."[332] Despite these seemingly conflicting strategy differences, Wikistrat analyst Dr. Michael Lumbers sees an American military presence in the Asia-Pacific region as necessary to support each of these alternatives.[333] The complex nature of military relations between the United States and China stems from concurrently and intermittently pursuing some of these contradictory strategies so that military relations are affected by the entire spectrum of options, from managing the rise of China into an international order that its leaders understand is beneficial to its interests, to remedying appeasement through unapologetic hard power, which still requires military dialogue to manage "security competition and friction in a way that supports overall stability."[334] As Chinese economic growth continues to slow and political, social, demographic, and environmental issues need addressing, the present reduction in size and professionalization of the People's Liberation Army (PLA) may offer an opportunity "to find face saving settlements for the disputes now churning across every domain."[335] Indeed, one way to accomplish this is through robust and mature military relationships, for which then-President Obama and Chinese President Xi Jinping had jointly called for in 2014 and 2015.[336] How the Trump administration will handle these relations is tenuous and may take time to unfold.

U.S. landpower will play a considerable role in managing this military relationship with China's land force-dominated defense leadership—and intra-land-force relations have been steadily improving despite recurring naval and air confrontations in the South China Sea.[337] For its part, USARPAC engages China through its open category, in which U.S.:

> legislative and policy constraints on defense relationships with these countries limit USARPAC's ability to directly engage them. . . . The countries themselves may have a policy to limit engagements with the U.S. military as a reflection of the state of the overall bilateral relationship. All of these factors limit USARPAC's engagement activities to senior level counterpart visits, medical, engineer, and HA/DR related exchanges—when allowed and where appropriate . . . USARPAC fosters responsible behavior through a focus on common security challenges and expands open lines of communication.[338]

Overcoming these limitations by developing "bilateral trust and transparency, the USARPAC Commander actively seeks opportunities to work with China in cooperative solutions to international security challenges."[339] Engagement and containment, even while at odds with each other, is crucial in order to contain crises and extend cooperative endeavors.[340] Current and previous PACOM Commanders, Admiral Harris and Admiral Samuel Locklear, have stressed fostering military relations with China even during heightened tensions to ensure communication and stability.[341] In the past, however, Chinese officials have used military contacts more as a signal of the state of diplomatic relations than as a tool to manage crises, although during a 2015 U.S. freedom of navigation operation close to Chinese occupied South China Sea features, the PLA used a defense telephone link concerning the incident.[342] A delicate balance of engagement is needed to continue such progress, even while "China is . . . both a recipient of security cooperation and a potential competitor driving some U.S. regional security cooperation efforts."[343]

The range of military engagement is circumscribed by the U.S. *National Defense Authorization Act of 2000*, which prohibits some activities and discussion of certain topics with Chinese forces that could create a national security risk; and China bars its members from attending any U.S. school, although military-to-military contacts are allowed.[344] Nonetheless, certain themes of engagement are important and drive the activities that ensue. For instance, senior leader dialogues are held to "develop common views on the international security environment and related challenges" in order to influence policy, cooperate on shared interests like counterterrorism and peacekeeping, and reduce tensions between the two states by improving operational safety and building institutional interactions.[345] Operational safety entails building confidence and reducing the perception of threat through such actions as the exchange of information concerning force size and composition, deployments and movement, exercises, and protocols governing chance meetings between forces.[346] To accomplish these goals, Defense One's analyst Kedar Pavgi reports that military-to-military contacts have climbed since a low point in

2010, consisting of only 7 military-to-military contacts, 5 of which were senior leader meetings, to about 25 in 2014, about half of which were exercise or educational contacts. Chinese-U.S. military contacts now seem less susceptible to being curtailed by adverse events, although whether that continues depends on relations established by the new Trump administration. Although the types of engagements are still clipped by policy and personality, they allow contacts from low-level exercises to cabinet secretary dialogues and are best categorized as senior leader visits and discussions, non-traditional operations exercises and training, education, and other engagements—examples of which are presented below.[347]

In terms of types and quantity of engagements, senior leader engagements are the most numerous, perhaps because they are the most reliable to control within legislative and policy restraints imposed by both sides. These high-level engagements include visits by the U.S. President, as Commander in Chief, to China in 2009 and 2014; bilateral discussions at international venues as occurred between the U.S. Secretary of Defense and PRC Minister of National Defense in Kuala Lumpur in 2015; and China's Chief of the General Staff of the PLA's visit to the United States in 2011.[348] Because land forces dominate the Chinese military structure, discussion between senior land force leaders are especially important, as when the U.S. Army Chief of Staff visited China in 2014. In addition to building personal and organizational relationships, these discussions should result in substantive agreements like the 2015 "army-to-army dialogue mechanism to better coordinate humanitarian assistance and disaster response practices."[349] High-level engagements concerning education are another permissible topic as witnessed during the Commandant of the USAWC's visit to the PLA's Academy of Military Science in Beijing in December 2015, or when the PLA's Peacekeeping Center discussed developing conceptual materials concerning peacekeeping and continuing their exchanges while visiting PKSOI at Carlisle Barracks in November 2015.[350] Such activities should result in more substantive engagement such as PLA officers attending the USAWC as international fellows, or U.S. Army and PLA forces serving together in United Nations peace operations.[351] Despite annual invitations, no PLA officer has ever attended the USAWC. In a small step toward closer peace operations, a U.S. Marine officer attended the Peacekeeping School in Beijing in 2015.[352] Although high-level relationships are essential, more opportunities for lower echelon personnel would give depth to engagement as ties mature slowly over time and repeated encounters. Former U.S. Ambassador to China and PACOM Commander Joseph Prueher related, "These personal relationships are more important than the formal agreements . . . [but] we don't have the amalgam that holds it together at the lower level."[353] Steady rotation of senior level U.S. officials to duties outside the region also detracts from more effective engagement.[354] U.S.-Chinese engagement continues apace especially among land forces, despite its detractors and slow results, because of its potential to enhance cooperation in areas that concern both countries, and reduce the potential for conflict between them—acting as a regional stability insurance policy.

One form of engagement where all levels of land force personnel can interact is non-traditional military operations, once referred to as military operations other than war. In order to better manage the competitive aspects of the Chinese relationship, the 2014 QDR recommends practical cooperation in a variety of areas including peacekeeping, disaster relief, and humanitarian assistance, which are major missions for U.S. landpower.[355] In order to burnish its image and gain practical experience, the PLA is investing heavily in these types of missions, which make a natural partnership between both forces, within the limits allowed them, because of the expertise and experience each side brings.[356] In disaster management, the two armies are conducting training and exercises "increasing in number and increasing in quality and scope . . . just short of a full-blown exercise."[357] For instance, in 2012, the PLA and U.S. Army held a tabletop HA/DR exercise in Chengdu; 60 PLA soldiers exercised with the National Guard in Hawaii in 2013; and, a Disaster Management Exchange was conducted on Hainan Dao in 2015, with about 200 soldiers from each side participating.[358] Also in that year, a trilateral survival exercise was held in the Australian Outback for the second year.[359] Although an observer since 2002, the PLA participated in the Cobra Gold exercises for the first time in 2014, but characteristically only in the humanitarian assistance portions.[360]

Another area of potential cooperation in which both armies have the expertise to share includes nation building, which "is one of the basic missions of the PLA . . . [and] a historic mission for the United States Army" offering natural venues to exchange ideas on civil-military relations, the role of the military in development, and domestic and international responsibilities.[361] Peace operations are another common interest between the two, and when coupled with nation building and HA/DR, could result in intriguing and substantive discussions over combined efforts to deal with failed or failing states, countering the proliferation of weapons of mass destruction and/or their effects, or preventing terrorism.[362] In the engineering realm, the U.S. Army Corps of Engineers oversees major river infrastructure projects that may be a valuable exchange with the Chinese who also deal with potential disasters along the Yangtze, Yellow, and other rivers, the peril of earthquakes to major cities, and how the destruction from each is mitigated.[363] Although engagements are now small and limited, with time they could prove a boon to both sides for the expertise exchanged, improvement in relations, and mitigation of the real consequences of disasters.

Another type of engagement, forward presence, may seem more difficult to derive benefits from with the PLA, but here too gains may be found. As with other states, high-level discussions, exercises, and training are each a part of forward presence engagement with China. However, compared to other South China Sea countries, these are sparse and lack any advantages of enduring interaction through personnel basing or prepositioning of equipment. Indeed, U.S. military forces' simultaneous engaging and deterring activities—congagement—makes forward positioning of U.S. personnel and equipment with partner countries an irritation to relations with China and a perceived security dilemma that the Chinese vigorously resist.[364] From a combat and deter perspective, U.S. forces in the region restrain Chinese options, as they are intended to do. However, if Chinese intentions are as cooperative as they claim, then current forward positioning of U.S. forces makes engagement stronger. U.S. forces in close proximity to China means that opportunities and duration to engage in exercises and training can increase, and it opens the door for multilateral interaction with the forces of countries not regularly encountered, as occurs during Cobra Gold. Some analysts claim that the U.S. forces presence in partner countries may also act "as a pacifier for the more aggressive impulses of American allies and partners in the region,"[365] much the same way that was an unofficial role of American land forces with their South Korean counterparts in the 1960s and 1970s. A detached view of the American presence in the region may see it as having a region-wide stabilizing effect of restraining aggression on both sides while offering venues to build confidence in one another and pursue common interests with the United States as a facilitator, and "over time can improve cooperation when policymakers are feeling friendly and reduce the chance of accidental clashes when policymakers are feeling prickly."[366] To date, the Chinese Government has been wary of such an approach, but if there were a breakthrough in such engagement, it would probably be led by the land forces.[367]

U.S. landpower's strategic role to engage states and shape conditions should limit the need for deterrence or combat if properly performed. Through security cooperation and engagement activities, regional states may better understand each other and ensure stability and security to address U.S. and other states' interests. U.S. landpower's contribution to this is to build partner capacity especially through interpersonal and organizational engagements with militaries dominated by their land forces, and engaged by regionally specialized U.S. land forces. Security cooperation activities help to develop friendly forces and interoperability through security assistance, the transfer of equipment and munitions, defense services, and education and training. Security cooperation through military-to-military engagement also takes the form of exercises and field training through programs like Pacific Pathways and exercises like Cobra Gold, non-traditional military and combat missions, and senior level and staff engagements through conferences and visits like PAMS and PALS. The forward presence of U.S. land forces through basing or prepositioning of equipment reinforces the strengths and advantages of shape and engage activities through enduring and recurring ties, and reassuring partners and warning adversaries of American commitment and resolve. USARPAC's levels of engagement are examples of the different intensities of interaction with other land forces including Vietnam, Malaysia, the Philippines, and even rival China. HA/DR and peace operations tend to be universally accepted cooperation activities, while combat maneuvers or actual operations, as with JSOTF-P, are reserved for close partners and allies. Engagement activities especially benefit ties with China, which is the most difficult and consequential of the relations, in order to build upon cooperation or mitigate crises. Thus of the three strategic U.S. landpower roles—combat and compel, deter and prevent, and engage and shape—the latter may be the most consequential in the disputes over the South China Sea.

RECOMMENDATIONS

The Chinese word for crisis is sometimes misperceived as composed of the characters for danger and opportunity based on common references ranging from former U.S. President John F. Kennedy's campaign speeches to the Nobel Peace Prize acceptance lecture by former U.S. Vice President Al Gore.[368] Despite being only partially accurate, this concept endures in the public mind as a useful touchstone for making necessary, if difficult, changes during chaotic times. The United States and East Asian countries are in a turbulent period where such opportunities exist, for good or ill. There is certainly much opportunity here for U.S. land forces to better support U.S. interests in the region, as described in this monograph. This section draws out, emphasizes, and elaborates on some of the findings and recommendations already presented as relevant for land forces in a semi-enclosed maritime environment concerning aspects of doctrine, operations, and engagement; organization; training and exercises, and material. Although examined in select categories, many of these recommendations are interdependent, so that some solutions are covered in other categories.

While significant opportunities may be grasped during uncertain times, there are risks to these proposed changes including long-time U.S. fiscal constraints on some of the material and operational recommendations, constraints that will probably endure despite recent American campaign rhetoric. Depending on how strict budgets become in addressing spending, the continuing low funding of U.S. land force personnel, units, and equipment will make their rebalance to Asia challenging and leave some of the recommendations here simply never-resourced requirements.[369] A bigger problem for these recommendations, and in the forming and managing of military and government policy of the future, is that no real American grand strategy has been articulated for a long time, which leaves military forces without an adequate foundation to organize, train, and equip forces, and vulnerable to competing priorities or half-measures if changes are started. Without the foundation of strategy and end states, the difficult trade-offs envisioned in this monograph between strengthening the security relationship with Vietnam, for example, with building trust and cooperation with China may come to naught as inconclusively debated or summarily reversed.[370] The first recommendations of this monograph then are to stabilize the policy environment through crafting a strategy to guide efforts and then establishing actionable budgets and guidance to attain strategic goals. Although these are obvious elements that have been long ignored, they are worth stating again. Even should these necessary tasks be completed, the implementation of changes in land force posture, methods of fighting and engaging, new and improving weapon systems, interoperability and interdependence, and personnel and training will not be easy in terms of foreign or domestic politics, but are necessary.[371] With all of these risks acknowledged, what follows are some recommendations to advance the role of U.S. land forces to fight, deter, or engage in support of national objectives and military operations in a semi-enclosed maritime environment, in general, and in the South China Sea in particular.

Within land force operations, several advances attained during nearly 2 decades of combat in dry land-locked battlefields need to be sustained because they are relatively inexpensive, powerful contributions to joint and interagency operations. First, maintain and strengthen the hard-won cooperation and interdependence between conventional Army and Marine forces with each other and with SOF in their complementary roles. As the demands of combat operations reduce, too often so does trust and cooperation among the land forces, as each seeks to protect service interests and budgets, while separating into garrison routines.

These stronger operational bonds may be taken for granted, which can happen without strong leadership and dedicated nurturing.

Also is the need to sustain and improve landpower's foundational role in enabling support to joint forces, to open and set the theater, provide logistics, establish wide area security, and other critical supporting contributions of landpower to air, sea, interagency, and partner organizations, which are often overlooked and thereby neglected in the interims between crises. Sustaining the knowledge, expertise, and capabilities that have been hard learned may require those skills and tasks to be streamlined and balanced for greater effectiveness. Lessons are expected from past and ongoing operations and should be applied to improve these critical capabilities especially since short notice operations and austere conditions are often encountered when U.S. forces deploy. These may be the most important landpower contributions to semi-enclosed maritime operations and should be reinforced.

One change to land force operations that will require organizational change and a doctrinal shift is fully integrating and controlling improved or to-be-developed landpower projection capabilities into the air and maritime domains. Overlapping weapon system threats and confined maneuvering areas fraught with physical hazards make semi-enclosed maritime environments particularly dangerous places for modern air and naval combat. This monograph proposed that land forces stationed in the littorals should project air, sea, and land fires into this environment to supplement air and naval power, or even provide the shield behind which air and sea power become a mobile reserve, counter strike force, or act as a deterrent. The specifics of these systems are discussed below, but to properly implement this concept, organizational and doctrinal changes are needed to fully integrate joint and combined systems through a cross-domain command and intelligence capability for collective regional defense. A mobile land-based C2 fires system for semi-enclosed maritime regions would fill a U.S. and partner capability gap that is especially apparent around the South China Sea.

A mobile land-based cross-domain C2 system would be less expensive, less vulnerable, larger and more capable, more available, and less provocative than similar air- or sea-based systems, and should include and sometimes depend upon partner country capabilities. Such an integrated system would defend air, sea, and land forces deploying to and operating in the theater, and enable joint force entry operations.[372] Adding maritime domain awareness capabilities as an early warning of changing events in the maritime domain would be a useful intelligence layer to build a common operating picture so that participating states could better coordinate responses. The current SEA Reassurance Fund could be used to integrate and develop the capabilities needed to build and employ this capability.[373] The U.S. Army would be responsible for providing many of the air-defense, surface-to-surface fires, and potentially land-based anti-ship and surveillance systems needed for the endeavor that may require adding and restructuring these elements and developing a scheme to deploy these units.[374] Operating the system in theater is a sign of resolve and ensures that hosting states are fully committed to the defense of the commons, including surveillance of piracy, terrorism, and other threats that would link the interests of regional states along with their systems. Doctrine, systems, and organization changes to realize this recommendation are needed, with research and acquisition necessary through U.S. and partner efforts. A fully integrated cross-domain C2 system is a much-needed capability to monitor and defend semi-enclosed maritime regions around the world, and a land-based system fully integrating partners is a practical choice.

The second change to land force operations that will require organizational and doctrinal change is developing a small-unit boat-based land force capable of patrolling and controlling littorals and intra-archipelagic waters. To counter gray zone tensions and nonstate actors' disruptive actions, growing more common in the South China Sea littoral, land forces require an "assured shallow-water maneuver capability [that] fills a tactical and operational need" to support defensive, offensive, stability, and humanitarian actions by land forces. Such a force properly trained and equipped could, for example, conduct raids or reconnaissance in the brown waters of a coastline or within the Spratly archipelago, as an example; provide counter-terrorism and other security services around friendly forces; interdict trafficking or pirates; and provide humanitarian services and disaster relief in shallow but navigable waterways or remote areas only accessible by such vessels. Since many of Southeast Asia's countries' problems are water-related, but its forces are land-centric, such a small-unit boat force is a natural engagement match with regional powers and thus satisfies the combat, deterrence, and engagement missions of U.S. land forces.[375] The Marine Corps is the best fit to perform this mission, but soldiers have conducted this task in the past and may have more personnel and capability to expand in this direction. Although this is a mission not conducted by U.S. forces since the Vietnam War, the obvious requirement and current uncertainty and changes in the political environment, both foreign and domestic, may now make this the time to consider instituting such capability.

Daily engagement and support to regional partners and allies is a powerful but relatively inexpensive way to achieve U.S. and regional partners' goals—a tool that needs to be strengthened. If, as Dr. David Lai of SSI contends, China's strategy mirrors the ancient Chinese game of *go*, then its recent moves of seizing the center of the board in the South China Sea through building up and militarizing the Spratly and Paracel Islands may be countered by the United States working the game board's edges, remaining fully engaged with Vietnam, Malaysia, the Philippines, and other involved regional powers.[376] In his inaugural address, however, President Trump may have signaled a weakening of support and engagement with like-minded partners when he proclaimed, "For many decades, we've enriched foreign industry at the expense of American industry, subsidized the armies of other countries while allowing for the very sad depletion of our military."[377] This monograph and other authorities believe that reducing engagement activities with key regional countries would ultimately be an expensive and debilitating mistake.[378] Instead, engagement should be increased and strengthened, with land forces in the lead, because of their stabilizing and defensive nature in a land forces-dominant region, as already presented. For reasons of its own new administration's policies, this may be particularly difficult to continue with the Philippines. However, even here, continuing influential ties and activities at lower echelons and in much-needed activities, below the headline levels of more fraught large exercises and equipment sales, are desirable to maintain personal relationships and force capabilities until official relationships allow more broad engagements again. While official relationships between the United States and the Philippines remain muted, landpower ties with the forces of Vietnam, Malaysia, Brunei, and Indonesia should be deepened. The Trump administration is already actively engaged in strengthening ties with Taiwan, perhaps playing an unexpected edge of the *go* game board.

Despite recent downgrading by the Philippines, training and exercising with Southeast Asian powers has been mutually beneficial, and should be maintained and diversified. International exercises like Cobra Gold allow states that might not otherwise engage with the United States or the Philippines, like China, to participate together in a variety of operating environments.[379] U.S. Army, Marine, and SOF each conduct their own bilateral exercises with regional states, often emphasizing particular missions or tasks of which USARPAC's Pacific Pathways program is an effective example of wisely engaging in various bilateral exercises, and should be continued. These bilateral exercises should concentrate on training activities sought after by partners. For instance, the U.S. Army could advance its cooperation in establishing a peacekeeping center with the VPA to the next level of running peacekeeping field and command post exercises or planning actual operations. The VPA is also interested in acquiring advanced field medical skills — with which U.S. land forces have much combat experience — and continuing urban search and rescue drills, all of which are examples of non-controversial ways to continue engagement despite Chinese protests. A more substantial step would be bolstering Vietnam's already capable amphibious forces through exercises and training with the U.S. Marine Corps. The Malaysian Army's nascent amphibious force would benefit too from increased training and exercise with the Marine Corps that the Malaysian Defense Minister appears to support.[380] For reasons such as these, the DoD needs to make sure that security cooperation remains an important tool for engagement despite possible political sentiment otherwise.

Engagement with more wary countries is both possible and necessary. The Philippine Army would also like to increase its abilities in peacekeeping, which is an entrée to which even the Duterte administration might not object, and could have the benefit of becoming a trilateral effort with Vietnam or perhaps even China. A more substantial but difficult activity would be to continue building the Philippine's air assault capability, which is much needed in its jungle and insular environment. Maintaining continuity in this and other U.S.-Philippines training and exercise efforts would be advantageous for Philippine forces but are uncertain in the current political environment. Relations with China have made military engagements, at the level described here, tenuous activities. Recent moves by the Trump administration have probably hampered any form of engagement for some time to come. Nonetheless, contact between U.S. and Chinese forces would at least reduce tensions, and the possibility for misunderstanding and miscalculations. U.S. land forces are the most likely to spearhead any future cooperation. Senior level military dialogues would air out challenges between the two sides and perhaps find some common views. As noted earlier by former U.S. Ambassador and USPACOM Commander Joseph Prueher, such personal relationships with Chinese officials "are more important than the formal agreements" and should be fostered.[381] The usual less contentious activities for relationships like this could re-establish ties including student exchanges, and practical cooperation in areas such as peacekeeping, HA/DR, and natural disaster mitigation and infrastructure projects in which both sides' land forces have much expertise.

Improvements to training and exercising are always necessary, but two main ideas are suggested here. Although joint and combined exercises like Cobra Gold are very useful, and single-service bilateral exercise can focus training for better results, more US-ARPAC exercises should include U.S. Marine and SOF elements in their exercises to maintain joint interoperability and increase access for the other services—and their exercises should do the same. A second suggestion comes from a 2016 USAWC study that recommends strengthening regional partner capacity with regional leaders like Australia and Japan, where the United States should assist in helping them develop regional defense operations through organizing and executing their own "Pathways" exercises. The report stated that:

> this initiative offers a unique opportunity for the participating nations to deepen cooperation and relationships among themselves . . . to increase regional military involvement and leadership among Asia-Pacific partners, providing regionally led security, stability, and cooperative defense.[382]

These proposed "Reverse Pathways" would not only increase and strengthen regional powers' capacities, but would also share some of the burdens of cooperation activities, and multiply the strands in the defense network of like-minded states as insurance against one relationship souring. For instance, recently difficult relations between the United States and the Philippines allow Japan to continue anchoring relations with the Philippines. Malaysian Defense Minister Hishammuddin Hussein has proposed that ASEAN "create a ready group that focuses on humanitarian assistance and disaster response capabilities," which is one form such an idea might take.[383]

Unit-to-unit engagement with regional states is a relatively inexpensive, rapid, and effective way to enhance access and operations in maritime environments, so expanding existing RAF and SPPs makes sense. Because of their importance as individual states and even more so as a bloc, the SPP should expand to cover all 10 ASEAN states to tighten their cooperation and collective actions.[384] Partnering with Malaysia and Brunei is especially important since both are directly impacted by the South China Sea disputes, and their officials have shown some interest in the program.[385] To increase stability and security in Southeast Asia, the SPP should focus on threats to stability and legitimacy including "disaster response, consequence management [CM], border and fixed site security, cyber defense, counter terrorism and counter trafficking," as well as improve partner resiliency in light of ongoing gray zone operations.[386] These focus areas are particularly well suited to the civil-military expertise that National Guard units bring to cooperative engagements, especially when interacting with civilian authorities.[387] A limited number of training days available to Guardsmen, however, has constrained this program and should be corrected through more resources, as intended by the Army Chief of Staff, or more innovative methods employed for engaging.[388]

Both the U.S. Army National Guard, through the SPP, and SOF have aligned their units to better understand a region—gaining practical expertise and insight. As former TRADOC Commander General Robert Cone emphasized, "if we can just get the first four brigades on the ground, anywhere we go, to be conversant in language, culture, and networks, then we will be far ahead of where we were in Iraq and Afghanistan."[389] To achieve such regional awareness, the U.S. Army and Marine Corps active forces and their reserves should be regionally aligned as well, to enhance combat and engagement actions, especially in HA/DR and foreign internal defense. Such customizing of RAF, initiated in the U.S. Army in 2012, is a challenge because many rival tasks compete for manpower, especially in a force as small as the Marine Corps. Assigning a continuum of scalable or smaller units to specialize and engage in a region would be one way to address this concern.[390] Although well intentioned, however, such alignments are prone to breaking down during the periods between crises, so an institutional change to keep personnel in units longer and to reassign them back to maintain regional focus should be considered, perhaps through a regimental system.[391] The U.S. Marine Corps, already notorious for splitting into East Coast and West Coast "tribes," may be further along such regional forces alignment than they think, especially with a large contingent of personnel permanently in Okinawa and Guam. Aligned forces must also be funded to exercise in their region and given the training needed to properly prepare for regular deployments and maintain their readiness.[392] Individual training to create specialists is also necessary to maintain regional expertise, ranging from the well-regarded Army Foreign Area Officer to the Strategic Broadening Seminar for non-commissioned and warrant officers.[393] Within the human domain, more culturally aware personnel, policies, and activities are crucial for landpower's effectiveness in combat and peacetime engagement, because, as respected SSI author Steven Metz concludes, "Most, if not all, U.S. military operations will continue to be cross-cultural."[394]

For deterrence and combat capabilities, a land-based cross-domain C2 system has already been proposed, but improvements to the joint and allied systems that are part of such an integrated network are needed. For instance, competent anti-air systems like Patriot and THAAD exist, but, as presented earlier, their capabilities need to be extended to cover the wider spaces of a maritime environment, and their capabilities need to be upgraded to counter the sophisticated A2AD systems fielded by the Chinese. Enough of these systems are not available for worldwide commitments, so more Patriot and THAAD air defense units are needed to protect vital U.S. bases in Okinawa, mainland Japan, and forward deployed bases that U.S. military forces might need in order to counter aggressive moves in the South China Sea.[395]

Anti-ship capabilities for U.S. land forces do not exist yet, but if pursued, as advocated by this monograph, making existing systems dual purpose for covering this mission is a good initial first step. The U.S. Army should fully pursue its programs of using the existing M777 155 mm howitzers to fire hypervelocity projectiles and the Excalibur precision guided munition for initial land-based mobile, short-range anti-ship weapons. In the longer term, the United States should work with partners like Japan and Vietnam, who are already developing anti-ship systems, to ensure interoperability in hardware, doctrine, and tactics, and C2 to attain an effective long-range anti-ship capability, which has U.S. Senate backing.[396]

ATACMS upgrade in range and ability to track slow-moving targets could cover much of the region's sea- and land-based threats out to 500 km when better integrated into a cross-domain C2 system. Such a system further complicates an aggressors plan and contributes to deterrence. However, such systems when fully fielded also increase offensive capability for land forces, which could be controversial internationally, and are significant expansions to roles, missions, and costs for land forces during fiscally constrained times, which could be controversial domestically.[397] Nonetheless, if the United States is serious about supporting its partners and allies around the world's littorals, and deterring aggression in the marginal seas, more funding, research, development, and acquisition are necessary.[398]

There are other recommendations suggested in this monograph that may be more practical in the long term than in the present political environment, so those are only covered briefly. Forward presence forces, temporary host-nation facilities, and prepositioned logistics sites are important tools for combat, deterrence, and engagement in order to reduce deployment time, costs, and vulnerability; show commitment in the region; and enhance interoperability, understanding, and networks with partners.[399] The Trump administration and some U.S. partners seem less interested in employing these force-enhancing tools; however, pursuing them should be done selectively with the hope for better prospects in the future. To compensate, forward-postured, sea-based land forces, such as the U.S. Marine Corps' Amphibious Readiness Groups' Marine Expeditionary Unit, should substitute when and where land-based forces lack access, as well as be properly funded to ensure availability and readiness for when such forces are needed.[400] Another postponed opportunity is greater engagement with Chinese forces. Without enhancing China's fighting capabilities, engagement on a variety of levels is needed to build relationships, understanding, and trust during crises and opportunities when these are needed. Despite political circumstances, engagement should continue as a fundamental aspect of the relationship, but the Chinese have used engagement as a carrot for their diplomatic purposes, and the Trump administration seems little inclined to use its soft power instruments with China. Nonetheless, as much engagement as may be salvaged should continue, in order to have some framework ready when political winds shift and engagement is needed again.[401]

CONCLUSION

U.S. landpower in the South China Sea is an essential component to stabilizing this contested region during America's strategic rebalance to the Asia-Pacific region. Together, the U.S. Army, Marine Corps, and SOF offer distinctive capabilities whose defensive nature in this semi-enclosed maritime environment tend to escalate less while still sending an unequivocal message of committed support and steady resolve to partners and competitors alike. The capabilities of U.S. landpower are also essential to augment other activities in the air, sea, and human domains in the South China Sea through direct support to diverse joint military operations, intergovernmental activities in pursuit of U.S. strategic interests, and in landpower's own engagement, deterrence, and strategic combat roles. U.S. landpower gives pause to states with aggressive intentions, creates networks that enhance abilities synergistically, and may also break down barriers to misunderstanding—all of which should result in a stabilizing role for U.S. landpower through its proper application in the South China Sea region.

To establish U.S. landpower as a critical part of security and stability in the region, this monograph presented how its wide-ranging capabilities have an important influence on the land and human domains rimming the South China Sea, and that directly support U.S. interests pursued by all of its government agencies. Even in a sea- and air-dominated environment, landpower's broad operational and strong support capabilities in pursuit of increasingly interdependent joint and unified operations make it an indispensable element in attaining U.S. interests. Landpower may be the most decisive, flexible, and versatile force through full spectrum operations, fully covering the range of military operations from humanitarian assistance to conventional state-on-state warfare, and is also crucial to understand, engage, and influence people and leaders. If the United States is to channel tensions in the region toward internationally acceptable forms of growth, prosperity, stability, and security, U.S. landpower holds special influence because land forces dominate this region's military structure. Landpower's capabilities are crucial for attaining the United States' national security interests of peace and stability in the South China Sea region.

The first of the strategic roles of landpower, to compel or fight and win decisively, is more important than is normally credited in a maritime environment. The U.S. Army provides indispensable support to other forces and agencies through its theater opening and sustaining abilities as lead military service in logistics, land transportation, communications, medical, and other support. Through its core competency of wide area security, the U.S. Army, often with the Marine Corps, is usually responsible for passive and active means to protect forces, populations, and infrastructure against external and internal threats. The Army's air and missile defense systems are particularly needed in this A2AD environment against pre-emptive strikes. The security role of sea control from the land through anti-ship missiles is a historic and influential one in a semi-enclosed sea environment, but still needs to be operationally developed by U.S. land forces. The counterland mission through surface-to-surface missiles acts as a shield to suppress close-in attack systems located around the region. Another core competency is combined arms maneuver. Amphibious operations, a mission assigned to all landpower forces, are a useful option during disasters and in the periphery of combat operations around the South China Sea. Maneuver by air offers another option but is also vulnerable in the current threat environment. Landpower's combat capability is a measure of last resort, but does give credibility to landpower's deter and engage strategic roles.

The second of the strategic roles of U.S. landpower, to deter and prevent war, is also crucial to stability in Southeast Asia. Credible U.S. deterrence in the region depends on the combat capabilities of U.S. landpower covered in this monograph. However, deterrence also needs to exhibit the will to back those capabilities, which is demonstrated through the forward presence of troops and prepositioning of equipment and supplies. The advantages of forward positioning can be gained through using hardened, dispersed, or temporary facilities. U.S. landpower's ability to help mitigate crises and contingencies, whether security related or natural or manmade disasters, is another means to show resolve and capability in the region, as demonstrated by JSOTF-P and JTF 505 operations in the Philippines. The importance of landpower to deterrence and preventing war is due to the resolve that land forces represent when committed by the U.S. Government, and the powerful influence landpower wields in the human aspects of military operations. With forward presence and operational interaction with the forces of Southeast Asia, U.S. forces have more opportunity to assure partners while improving host nation military capabilities and interoperability through the shaping and engagement actions of security cooperation.

U.S. landpower's strategic role to engage states and shape conditions may well reduce the need for deterrence or combat. Through security cooperation and engagement activities, regional states may better understand each other and ensure stability and security to address U.S. and regional states' interests. U.S. landpower builds partner capacity through interpersonal and organizational engagements with militaries dominated by their land forces. Security cooperation activities also help to develop the capabilities of friendly forces and regional interoperability through security assistance, equipment, defense services, and education to partners from the United States. Security cooperation also takes the form of exercises and field training, military-to-military engagement exercises, non-traditional military and combat missions, and senior level and staff engagements. The forward presence of U.S. land forces reinforces the strengths and advantages of shaping and engagement activities for which multiple examples were given for Vietnam, Malaysia, the Philippines, and even rival China in a manner in which ties become more enduring and recurring. Although all three of the U.S. landpower strategic roles—combat and compel, deter and prevent, and engage and shape—are mutually dependent upon each other, engage and shape may be the most important in stabilizing the disputes in the South China Sea.

The use of landpower to address the disputes in the South China Sea is not usually considered in what is typically labeled a maritime- and air-centric theater, but the role of U.S. landpower is profound in this arena. Should the situation come to conflict, sea and air power may be the "big stick" of fighting in the South China Sea region with U.S. landpower support, but it is landpower that will speak softly, and its influence will be undeniable in deterring war or, should that fail, winning the peace.

ENDNOTES

1. The author gratefully acknowledges the support and help he received for this monograph from his colleagues: Commander (Ret.) David M. Birdwell, Colonel (Ret.) John A. Bonin, Colonel (Ret.) Donald Boose, Colonel (Ret.) William G. Braun, Colonel Stephen C. Ma, Colonel (Ret.) Michael A. Marra, and Colonel (Ret.) Brett D. Weigle.

2. The Air-Sea Battle concept has been subsumed into the *Joint Concept for Access and Maneuver in the Global Commons* (JAM-GC) in recognition of the joint and integrated nature of modern U.S. military operations, as explained later in this monograph, and gradual acknowledgement of the influence of landpower in semi-enclosed maritime environments like the South China Sea. Harry J. Kazianis, "Air-Sea Battle's Next Step: JAM-GC on Deck," *The National Interest*, November 25, 2015, available from *nationalinterest.org/feature/air-sea-battles-next-step-jam-gc-deck-14440*, accessed February 7, 2015; and Lieutenant Colonel Jason B. Nicholson and Joseph Trevithick, "The Army's New Role in the Pacific Pivot," *Proceedings: U.S. Naval Institute*, Vol. 141, No. 10, October 2015, pp.

60-65, available from *www.usni.org/magazines/proceedings/2015-10/ armys-new-role-pacific-pivot*, accessed January 20, 2016.

3. China added approximately 4.69 square miles to the Spratly Islands in 2014 and 2015 through its impressive but destructive land reclamation efforts, while Vietnam, Malaysia, the Philippines, and Taiwan together added only about 0.34 square miles in the past 40 years. Clarence J. Bouchat, *Dangerous Ground: The Spratly Islands and U.S. Interests and Approaches*, Carlisle, PA: Strategic Studies Institute, U.S. Army War College, 2013, p. 3, available from *ssi.armywarcollege.edu/pubs/display.cfm?pubID=1187*, accessed March 4, 2016; Christopher P. Cavas, "US Pacific Chief Talks China, Regional Partnerships," DefenseNews.com, January 27, 2016, available from *www.defensenews.com/story/defense/naval/ navy/2016/01/27/harris-pacific-command-south-china-sea-naval-artificial-islands-reefs-india-thailand-japan-korea-philippines/79423764/*, accessed February 19, 2016; and Clarence J. Bouchat; *The Paracel Islands and U.S. Interests and Approaches in the South China Sea*, Carlisle, PA: Strategic Studies Institute, U.S. Army War College, 2014, p. 3, available from *ssi.armywarcollege.edu/pubs/display. cfm?pubID=1207*, accessed March 4, 2016.

4. John R. Deni, *The Future of American Landpower: Does Forward Presence Still Matter? The Case of the Army in the Pacific*, Carlisle, PA: Strategic Studies Institute, U.S. Army War College, June 2014, p. 2, available from *ssi.armywarcollege.edu/pubs/display. cfm?pubID=1202*, accessed February 13, 2016; and Michael Green, Kathleen Hicks, and Mark Cancian, dirs., *Asia-Pacific Rebalance 2025: Capabilities, Presence, and Partnerships: An Independent Review of U.S. Defense Strategy in the Asia-Pacific*, Washington, DC: Center for Strategic and International Studies, January 2016, p. 131, available from *csis.org/files/publication/160119_Green_AsiaPacificRebalance2025_Web_0.pdf*, accessed January 29, 2016. Disregarding the sub-unified command in Korea that has long been held by a U.S. Army General (four-star), this is an important adjustment in rank conscious Asian societies.

5. Office of the Secretary of Defense, *Quadrennial Defense Review 2014*, Washington, DC: U.S. Department of Defense, March 4, 2014, p. 34, available from *archive.defense.gov/pubs/2014_Quadrennial_Defense_Review.pdf*, accessed January 25, 2016.

6. Gordon Lubold and Trefor Moss, "Aboard U.S. Ship in South China Sea, Defense Secretary Invokes 'Big Stick'," *The Wall Street Journal*, November 5, 2015, available from *www.wsj.com/ articles/aboard-u-s-ship-in-south-china-sea-defense-secretary-invokes-big-stick-1446720866*, accessed February 1, 2016.

7. Headquarters, Department of the Army (HQDA), *The Army*, Army Doctrinal Publication (ADP) 1, Chg. No. 1, Washington, DC: U.S. Government Printing Office, September 17, 2012, p. 1-4, available from *https://www.army.mil/e2/c/downloads/303969. pdf*, accessed January 16, 2016.

8. There is no joint forces definition of "landpower," see Joint Chiefs of Staff, *DOD Dictionary of Military and Associated Terms*, Joint Reference Publication, Washington, DC: U.S. Department of Defense, March 2017, available from *www.dtic.mil/doctrine/dod_ dictionary*, accessed April 13, 2017; Glenn K. Cunningham, "Landpower in Traditional Theory and Contemporary Application," in J. Boone Bartholomees, Jr., ed., *U.S. Army War College Guide to National Security Policy and Strategy, 2nd ed.*, Carlisle, PA: Strategic Studies Institute, U.S. Army War College, 2006, p. 163, available from *ssi.armywarcollege.edu/pubs/display.cfm?pubID=708*, accessed January 17, 2016.

9. Cunningham, p. 163; Joint Chiefs of Staff, *Joint Operations*, Joint Publication (JP) 3-0, Washington, DC: U.S. Department of Defense, January 17, 2017, p. V-13, available from *www.dtic.mil/ doctrine/new_pubs/jp3_0_20170117.pdf*, accessed April 13, 2017, lists the six operational planning phases as: Phase 0 Shape, Phase I Deter, Phase II Seize the Initiative, Phase III Dominate, Phase IV Stabilize, Phase V Enable Civil Authority. The environmental domains of military power include land, sea, air, space, cyberspace, and a more recently debated human domain. Joint operations are the interoperable and interdependent use of the U.S. Army, Navy, Air Force, and Marine Corps toward common national goals.

10. Raymond T. Odierno, James F. Amos, and William H. McRaven, *Strategic Landpower: Winning the Clash of Wills*, Washington, DC: The Pentagon, 2013, p. 5, available from *www. tradoc.army.mil/FrontPageContent/Docs/Strategic%20Landpower%20 White%20Paper.pdf*, accessed January 12, 2016.

11. U.S. Army Special Operations Command (SOCOM), *AR-SOF Operating Concept 2022*, Fort Bragg, NC: U.S. Special Operations Command, September 26, 2014, p. 5, available from *www.soc.mil/Assorted%20Pages/ARSOF%20Operating%20Concept%20 2014.pdf*, accessed January 19, 2016; and Harry B. Harris, Jr., "Role of Land Forces In Ensuring Access To Shared Domains," public speech to Land Power in the Pacific (LANPAC) Symposium 2016, Sheraton, Waikiki, Hawaii, May 25, 2016, available from *www.pacom.mil/Media/SpeechesTestimony/tabid/6706/Article/781889/lan-pac-symposium-2016-role-of-land-forces-in-ensuring-access-to-shared-domains.aspx*, accessed June 9, 2016.

12. David Knych, "Preserving the U.S. Army's Land Combat Power," in Samuel R. White, Jr., ed., *Futures Seminar: the United States Army in 2025 and Beyond,* Vol. 2, Carlisle Barracks, PA: Center for Strategic Leadership, U.S. Army War College, December 2015, p. 37, available from *http://publications.armywarcollege.edu/ pubs/2972.pdf*, accessed January 15, 2016.

13. Lukas Milevski, "Fortissimus Inter Pares: The Utility of Landpower in Grand Strategy," *Parameters*, Vol. 42, No. 2, July 2012, p. 6, available from *ssi.armywarcollege.edu/pubs/parameters/ Articles/2012summer/Milevski.pdf*, accessed January 21, 2016.

14. U.S. Army SOCOM, pp. 1, 5; John M. McHugh and Raymond T. Odierno, *2012 Army Posture: The Nation's Force of Decisive Action*, posture statement to the Committees and Subcommittees of the United States Senate and the House of Representatives, 2nd Sess., 112th Cong., Washington, D.C., February 2012, p. 22, available from *www.army.mil/e2/rv5_downloads/aps/aps_2012.pdf*, accessed February 29, 2016; and HQDA, *The Army*, p. 1-1.

15. Douglas Ollivant, "Go Army, Beat Navy," *Foreign Policy*, September 28, 2012, available from *foreignpolicy.com/2012/09/28/ go-army-beat-navy/*, accessed February 14, 2015.

16. Odierno, Amos, and McRaven, p. 7.

17. The term "decisive action" replaced the term "full spectrum operations" as the concept of continuous, simultaneous offense, defense, stability, or defense support of civil authorities. The term "full spectrum operations" continues to be used in this

monograph, however, as it is more illustrative for its audience. HQDA, Training and Doctrine Command (TRADOC), *Unified Land Operations*, ADP 3-0, Washington, DC: U.S. Government Printing Office, October 10, 2011, p. 5, available from *https://www.army.mil/e2/rv5_downloads/info/references/ADP_3-0_ULO_Oct_2011_APD.pdf*.

18. Robert B. Brown and Ronald W. Sprang, *Human Domain: Essential to Victory in Future Operations*, White Paper, Fort Benning, GA: U.S. Army Maneuver Center of Excellence, n.d., p. 5; and Cunningham, p. 165.

19. HQDA, *The Army*, p. 1-4.

20. Francis G Hoffman, "What the QDR Ought to Say about Landpower," *Parameters*, Vol. 43, No. 4, Winter 2013-14, p. 7, available from *ssi.armywarcollege.edu/pubs/Parameters/Issues/Winter_2013/TheQuarterly_Winter2013-14_v43n4.pdf*, accessed January 11, 2016; and U.S. Department of the Navy (USDN), *Marine Corps Operations*, Marine Corps Doctrinal Publication (MCDP) 1-0, Washington, DC: Headquarters, U. S. Marine Corps, August 9, 2011, p. 1-3, available from *www.marines.mil/Portals/59/Publications/MCDP%201-0%20Marine%20Corps%20Operations.pdf*, accessed January 18, 2016.

21. Figure sourced from Cunningham, p. 166.

22. Odierno, Amos, and McRaven, p. 3; HQDA, *The Army*, p. 1-1; and Brown and Sprang, pp. 2, 5-6. Note: that as a human contrived environment one could also argue that cyberspace should be included in this discussion. While probably true, including cyberspace into the discussion goes beyond the scope of this monograph.

23. Charles T. Cleveland, Shaw S. Pick, and Stuart L. Farris, "Shedding Light on the Gray Zone: A New Approach to Human-Centric Warfare," *Army*, Vol. 65, No. 9, September 2015, p. 21, available from *https://www.ausa.org/articles/shedding-light-gray-zone-new-approach-human-centric-warfare*, accessed January 16, 2015.

24. Frank Hoffman and Michael C. Davies, "Joint Force 2020 and the Human Domain: Time for a New Conceptual Framework?" *Small Wars Journal*, Vol. 9, No. 6, June 10, 2013, available from *smallwarsjournal.com/jrnl/art/joint-force-2020-and-the-human-domain-time-for-a-new-conceptual-framework*, accessed January 16, 2016.

25. Charles T. Cleveland and Stuart L. Farris, "Toward Strategic Landpower," *Army*, July 2013, pp. 21-22, available from *www.ausa.org/publications/armymagazine/archive/2013/07/Documents/Cleveland_July2013ARMY.pdf*, accessed January 11, 2016; Steven Metz, "Strategic Landpower Task Force Research Report," *Newsletter*, Strategic Studies Institute, U.S. Army War College, October 2013, available from *ssi.armywarcollege.edu/index.cfm/articles//STRATEGIC-LANDPOWER-TASK-FORCE/2013/10/3*, accessed January 11, 2016; and quote from Sydney J. Freedberg, Jr., "After '10 Years of Abject Failure,' Army, SOCOM, Marine Leaders Focus on 'Strategic Landpower'," Breaking Defense, August 27, 2013, available from *breakingdefense.com/2013/08/10-years-of-abject-failure-army-socom-marine-leaders-focus-on-strategic-landpower/*, accessed January 18, 2016.

26. Grant M. Martin, "The Sublime: The Paradox of the 7th Warfighting Function," *Small Wars Journal*, Vol. 9, No. 11, November 25, 2013, available from *smallwarsjournal.com/jrnl/art/the-sublime-the-paradox-of-the-7th-warfighting-function*, accessed January 16, 2016; Hoffman and Davies; William T. Johnsen, *Toward a Theory of Landpower for the 21st Century*, Carlisle Baracks, PA: U.S. Army War College, 2015, p. 14; and Freedberg, Jr., "After '10 Years of Abject Failure'"; Steven Metz in his report covers the pros and cons of formally institutionalizing the human domain as a concept, see Metz.

27. At the time of publication, the term "human domain," while controversial, is better known and understood and will be used for this concept in this monograph. William G. Braun, Professor of Practice at the U.S. Army War College's (USAWC) Strategic Studies Institute (SSI), written comments to the present author, July 15, 2016.

28. Hoffman and Davies; Metz; Bennet S. Sacolick and Wayne W. Grigsby, Jr., "Special Operations/Conventional Forc-

es Interdependence: A Critical Role in 'Prevent, Shape, Win'," *Army*, June 2012, p. 40, available from *www.ausa.org/publications/armymagazine/archive/2012/06/Documents/Sacolick_0612.pdf*, accessed February 11, 2016; and U.S. Army Pacific Command (USARPAC), *Partnering in the Pacific Theater: Assuring Security and Stability through Strong Army Partnerships*, Fort Shafter, HI: U.S. Army Pacific Command, September 26, 2014, p. 11, available from *www.usarpac.army.mil/pdfs/Partnering%20in%20the%20Pacific%20Theater.pdf*, accessed January 26, 2016.

29. Hoffman, p. 10.

30. Green *et al.*, pp. 132-133.

31. Odierno, Amos, and McRaven, pp. 5-6; and U.S. Army SO-COM, p. 7.

32. HQDA, TRADOC, *Unified Land Operations*, p. 5; and John A. Bonin, "Roles and Responsibilities of an Army Service Command Component," presentation slides, Center for Strategic Leadership (CSL), U.S. Army War College, Carlisle Barracks, PA, August 19, 2015, slide 3.

33. Michael Orzetti, "Extinct Force 21: EF 21's Existential Threat to the Marine Corps," *Marine Corps Gazette*, Vol. 99, No. 12, December 2015, p. 27.

34. Matthew Shenberger, *Strategic Decision Space: the Marine Corps in the 21st Century*, Strategy Research Project, Carlisle Barracks, PA: U.S. Army War College, 2013, pp. 13-14, available from *www.hsdl.org/?view&did=720097*, accessed January 18, 2016.

35. U.S. Army Special Operations Forces (SOF) includes Special Forces (Green Berets), Rangers, and Civil Affairs with aviation, logistics, and information support elements; and U.S. Marine Corps SOF include Raiders and their support elements.

36. Joint Chiefs of Staff, *Special Operations*, JP 3-05, Washington, DC: U.S. Department of Defense, July 16, 2014, p. ix, available from *www.dtic.mil/doctrine/new_pubs/jp3_05.pdf*, accessed April 13, 2017.

37. *Ibid.*, I-7.

38. USDN, p. 2-16.

39. Green *et al.*, pp. 135-136.

40. Metz.

41. Brown and Sprang, p. 2.

42. HQDA, *The Army*, p. 3-2.

43. William T. Johnsen, *Re-Examining the Roles of Landpower in the 21st Century and Their Implications*, Carlisle, PA: Strategic Studies Institute, U.S. Army War College, November 2014, p. 17, available from *ssi.armywarcollege.edu/pubs/display.cfm?pubID=1237*, accessed January 16, 2016.

44. Joint Chiefs of Staff, *Joint Operational Access Concept (JOAC)*, Joint Concepts, Washington, DC: U.S. Department of Defense, January 2012, pp. i, 16-17, available from *www.dtic.mil/doctrine/concepts/joint_concepts/joac_2012.pdf*, accessed April 13, 2017.

45. HQDA, TRADOC, *Unified Land Operations*, p. 7.

46. Scott Katrosh, "A General Purpose Fighting Force: The Foundation to Win in the Complex World of the 21st Century," in Samuel R. White, Jr., ed., *Futures Seminar: the United States Army in 2025 and Beyond*, Vol. 2, Carlisle Barracks, PA: Center for Strategic Leadership, U.S. Army War College, December 2015, p. 26, available from *https://csl.armywarcollege.edu/usacsl/publications/FuturesElectiveCompendium(Vol%202%20-%202015).pdf*, accessed January 15, 2016.

47. Knych, p. 35; and HQDA, TRADOC, *The U.S. Army Operating Concept: Win in a Complex World, 2020-2040*, Pamphlet 525-3-1, Washington, DC: U.S. Government Printing Office, October 31, 2014, p. 10, available from *https://www.tradoc.army.mil/tpubs/pams/tp525-3-1.pdf*, accessed January 12, 2016.

48. Barack Obama, *The National Security Strategy of the United States of America*, Washington, DC: The White House, February

2015, p. 2, available from *https://obamawhitehouse.archives.gov/sites/ default/files/docs/2015_national_security_strategy.pdf*, accessed April 17, 2017. The 2010 national interests were the same as these interests stated in 2015.

49. Office of the Secretary of Defense, p. v.

50. Leon Panetta, *Sustaining U.S. Global Leadership: Priorities for 21st Century Defense*, Washington, DC: U.S. Department of Defense, January 2012, available from *www.defense.gov/news/Defense_ Strategic_Guidance.pdf*, accessed January 8, 2016.

51. Panetta, p. 3; Michael W. King, *United States and the Spratly Islands: Six Actors, Which Stage?* Strategy Research Project, Carlisle Barracks, PA: U.S. Army War College, 2002, p. 20, available from *oai.dtic.mil/oai/oai?verb=getRecord&metadataPrefix=html&identifier= ADA401876*, accessed January 20, 2016; and Thomas J. Bickford, Lisa Hannett, Edward Skolnick, and Albert S. Willner, *The Role of the U.S. Army in Asia*, Arlington, VA: Center for Naval Analysis, May 2015, p. 17, available from *https://www.cna.org/CNA_files/ PDF/CRM-2015-U-010431-Final.pdf*, accessed March 10, 2016.

52. Bickford *et al.*, p. 17; and Michael McDevitt, "U.S. Policy in East Asia: East Asian Maritime Disputes," briefing slides and lecture, U.S. Army War College, Carlisle Barracks, PA, January 7, 2016, slide 2.

53. Joint Chiefs of Staff, *The National Military Strategy of the United States of America: 2011 Redefining America's Military Leadership*, Washington, DC: U.S. Department of Defense, February 2011, p. 7, available from *www.defense.gov/Portals/1/Documents/ pubs/2011-National-Military-Strategy.pdf*, accessed March 10, 2016.

54. Guy Brynt Parmeter, *The Strategic Shift to the Asia-Pacific and the U.S. Army*, Strategy Research Project, Carlisle Barracks, PA: U.S. Army War College, 2012, pp. 11, 17, available from *handle.dtic.mil/100.2/ADA561837*, accessed April 17, 2017.

55. Odierno, Amos, and McRaven, p. 4.

56. *Ibid.*

57. *Ibid.*; and Brian J. Stokes, *Prevent, Promote, and Hedge: US Military Power in the South China Sea*, Civilian Research Project, Carlisle Barracks, PA: U.S. Army War College, 2012, pp. 18-19, available from *www.dtic.mil/dtic/tr/fulltext/u2/a592509.pdf*, accessed February 12, 2016.

58. Headquarters, United States Pacific Command (USPACOM), "About USPACOM," n.d., available from *www.pacom.mil/About-USPACOM/*, accessed April 17, 2017.

59. *Ibid.*

60. Stokes, p. 6; and Kimberly Field and Stephan Pikner, "The Role of U.S. Land Forces in the Asia-Pacific," *Joint Force Quarterly*, Vol. 74, 3rd Qtr., 2014, available from *ndupress.ndu.edu/Media/News/News-Article-View/Article/577525/jfq-74-the-role-of-us-land-forces-in-the-asia-pacific/*, accessed February 14, 2016; Ollivant; and Chen Jimin, "Messages from the U.S. 2015 National Security Strategy Report," *China-U.S. Focus*, April 5, 2015, available from *www.chinausfocus.com/peace-security/messages-from-the-u-s-2015-national-security-strategy-report*, accessed April 21, 2017.

61. Parmeter, pp. 7-9; and Nishant Dahiya, "Trump and China: Intentionally Provocative or Unprepared?" National Public Radio, *Morning Edition*, January 17, 2017, available from *www.npr.org/sections/parallels/2017/01/17/510116169/trump-and-china-intentionally-provocative-or-unprepared?utm_source=Sailthru&utm_medium=email&utm_campaign=Early%20Bid%20Brief:%2001.18.2017&utm_term=Editorial%20-%20Military%20-%20Early%20Bird%20Brief*, accessed January 18, 2016.

62. Li Mingjiang, "Cooperation for Competition: China's Approach to Regional Security in East Asia," in Wilhelm Hofmeister, ed., *Security Politics in Asia and Europe*, Panorama: Insights Into Asian and European Affairs Occasional Papers Series, No. 2, Singapore: Konrad Adenauer Stiftung, 2010, pp. 121-123, 126-127, available from *www.kas.de/upload/dokumente/2010/06/PolDi-Asien_Panorama_02-2010/Panorama_2-2010_SecurityPolitics_Li.pdf*, accessed January 16, 2016; Shashank T. Upasani, *Exploring Options to Address China's Strategy in South Asia*, Strategy Research Project, Carlisle Barracks, PA: U.S. Army War College, 2013, p. 36, available from *oai.dtic.mil/oai/oai?verb=getRecord&metadataPrefix=html&identifier=ADA590266*, accessed March 1, 2016; and

Ben Lowsen, "How China Fights: The PLA's Strategic Doctrine," Asia Defense, blog of *The Diplomat*, April 6, 2016, available from *thediplomat.com/2016/04/how-china-fights-the-plas-strategic-doctrine/*, accessed April 6, 2016.

63. Parmeter, pp. 14-15; Kedar Pavgi, "Here's One Way the US-China Relationship Is Improving," Defense One, August 4, 2015, available from *www.defenseone.com/politics/2015/08/heres-one-way-us-china-relationship-improving/118865/*, accessed February 19, 2016; Bickford *et al.*, p. 17; and Lowsen.

64. Green *et al.*, pp. 12-13; and Pavgi.

65. Peter Gadd, *Rebalance to the Pacific: Resourcing the Strategy*, Strategy Research Project, Carlisle Barracks, PA: U.S. Army War College, 2013, p. 17, available from *oai.dtic.mil/oai/oai?verb=getRecord&metadataPrefix=html&identifier=ADA589241*, accessed February 1, 2016; Field and Pikner; and Robert Chamberlain, "Back to reality: Why land power trumps in the national rebalance toward Asia," *Armed Forces Journal*, May 1, 2013, available from *www.armedforcesjournal.com/back-to-reality/*, accessed April 25, 2016.

66. Phil Stewart and Patricia Zengerle, "Trump's Pentagon choice says U.S. needs to be ready to confront Russia," Reuters, January 12, 2017, available from *www.reuters.com/article/us-usa-congress-mattis-idUSKBN14W1KK*, accessed January 14, 2017.

67. Upasani, pp. 1-3; and Stokes, p. 7.

68. Mark A. Olsen, *Landpower in Asia — Historical Insights for the Pivot to the Pacific*, Fort Leavenworth, KS: School of Advanced Military Studies, U.S. Army Command and General Staff College, 2013, p. 24, available from *www.dtic.mil/cgi-bin/GetTRDoc?AD=ADA589096*, accessed February 14, 2016.

69. Lowsen.

70. Joseph Bosco, "How Obama Can Deter China," Real Clear World, September 23, 2015, available from *www.realclearworld.com/articles/2015/09/23/obama_taiwan_deter_china_111455.html*, accessed January 26, 2016; and Tanguy Struye De Swielande, "The Reassertion of the United States in the Asia-Pacific Region,"

Parameters, Vol. 42, No. 1, Spring 2012, pp. 77-78, available from *ssi.armywarcollege.edu/pubs/parameters/Articles/2012spring/Struye_de_Swielande.pdf*, accessed March 9, 2016.

71. Shannon Tiezzi, "Yes, the US Does Want to Contain China (Sort of)," China Power, blog of *The Diplomat*, August 8, 2015, available from *thediplomat.com/2015/08/yes-the-us-does-want-to-contain-china-sort-of/*, accessed February 4, 2015.

72. Stokes, pp. 1, 9.

73. HQDA, TRADOC, *The U.S. Army Operating Concept*, pp. 12-13.

74. Mira Rapp-Hooper, "Six Summertime Steps in the South China Sea," War on the Rocks, August 6, 2015, available from *https://warontherocks.com/2015/08/six-summertime-steps-in-the-south-china-sea-2/*, accessed February 4, 2016; Chamberlain; June Teufel Dreyer, "The Rise of China and the Geopolitics of East Asia," *Orbis*, Vol. 59, Iss. 4, Fall 2015, p. 529; Kurt Campbell and Brian Andrews, *Explaining the U.S. 'Pivot' to Asia*, London: Chatham House, August 1, 2013, p. 3; and Sydney J. Freedberg, Jr., "Reshape US Army, Asian Alliances to Deter China: CSBA," Breaking Defense, February 3, 2016, available from *breakingdefense.com/2016/02/reshape-us-army-asian-alliances-to-deter-china-csba/*, accessed February 6, 2016.

75. Nathan P. Freier, auth., Daniel Bilko, Matthew Driscoll, Akhil Iyer, Walter Rugen, Terrence Smith, Matthew Trollinger, contrib. auth., Maren Leed, dir., *U.S. Ground Force Capabilities through 2020*, Washington, DC: Center for Strategic and International Studies, 2011, p. 42, available from *csis.org/files/publication/111116%20-%20Freier_USGroundForces_Web.pdf*, accessed February 2, 2016; and Dreyer, pp. 518, 524.

76. Deni, *The Future of American Landpower*, pp. 20-21; David W. Barno, Nora Bensahel, and Travis Sharp, "Pivot but Hedge: A Strategy for Pivoting to Asia While Hedging in the Middle East," *Orbis*, Vol. 56, Iss. 2, Spring 2012, p. 161; and Green *et al.*, p. 3.

77. Bickford *et al.*, p. 29; Li, p. 126; Lubold and Moss; and Sydney J. Freedberg, Jr., "What Lessons Do China's Island Bases Offer the US Army," Breaking Defense, May 5, 2016, available

from *breakingdefense.com/2016/05/chinese-island-bases-show-the-way -for-us-army/*, accessed May 10, 2016. For a complete discussion of the concept of coercive gradualism, see William G. Pierce, Douglas G. Douds, and Michael A. Marra, "Understanding Coercive Gradualism," *Parameters*, Vol. 45, No. 3, Autumn 2015, pp. 51-61, available from *ssi.armywarcollege.edu/pubs/ Parameters/issues/Autumn_2015/Parameters%20Autumn%20 2015%20Vol45%20No3_ONLINE.pdf*, accessed February 19, 2016.

78. Dreyer, p. 525; and Lee Jaehyon, "China is Recreating the American 'Hub-and-Spoke' System in Asia," Flashpoints, blog of *The Diplomat*, September 11, 2015, available from *thediplomat. com/2015/09/china-is-recreating-the-american-hub-and-spoke-system- in-asia/*, accessed February 5, 2016.

79. USARPAC, *Partnering in the Pacific*, p. 7; Bickford *et al.*, pp. 17, 41-42; Field and Pikner; and Deni, *The Future of American Landpower*, p. 2.

80. Odierno, Amos, and McRaven, p. 9.

81. Braun, written comments to the present author, July 15, 2016.

82. Freedberg, Jr., "Reshape US Army, Asian Alliances to Deter China"; and Bickford *et al.*, p. 44.

83. John R. Deni, "Strategic Landpower in the Indo-Asia-Pa-cific," *Parameters*, Vol. 43, No. 3, Autumn 2013, pp. 77, 82, available from *ssi.armywarcollege.edu/pubs/Parameters/Issues/Autumn_2013/ Parameters_Autumn2013_v43n3.pdf*, accessed February 13, 2016; and Chamberlain.

84. HQDA, *The Army*, pp. 1-2, 1-6; and quote from Field and Pikner.

85. This was also true in 2012, but Taiwan's Chief was an Air Force officer, and Indonesia's Chief a navy officer — only the third non-Army appointment in 70 years. USARPAC, *Partnering in the Pacific*, pp. 2, 23; and IHS Markit, "Jane's Military and Security Assessments Intelligence Centre," available from *https://www. ihs.com/products/janes-military-security-assessments.html*, accessed April 18, 2017.

86. Field and Pikner.

87. Barno, Bensahel, and Sharp, pp. 174-175.

88. Parmeter, p. 12; and Chamberlain.

89. Freier *et al.*, *U.S. Ground Force Capabilities*, p. vii.

90. *Ibid.*; U.S. Army SOCOM, p. 20; and Joint Chiefs of Staff, *Special Operations*, p. I-2.

91. USDN, p. 1-2; Parmeter, pp. 12-13; Bickford *et al.*, pp. 41-42, 56-57; and Green *et al.*, p. 29.

92. Olsen, p. 19.

93. Green *et al.*, p. 16; and Field and Pikner. Although Air-Sea Battle may no longer be the official name, it is a valid term and more expressive than the official term JAM-GC, so it is purposefully used here.

94. Lubold and Moss.

95. Freedberg, Jr., "Reshape US Army, Asian Alliances to Deter China."

96. Deni, *The Future of American Landpower*, pp. 25-27.

97. McDevitt, "U.S. Policy in East Asia," slide 30.

98. USARPAC, *Partnering in the Pacific*, p. 1; and John A. Bonin, Professor of Concepts and Doctrine, Center for Strategic Leadership (CSL), U.S. Army War College, Carlisle Barracks, PA, April 8, 2016, e-mail discussion with the present author.

99. Bickford *et al.*, p. iii.

100. The 2016 report rated the South China Sea's conflict potential as both high impact and high likelihood, but lowered its likelihood in its 2017 report. Paul Stares, *Preventive Priorities Survey, 2017*, Washington, DC: Council on Foreign Relations, 2017, p. 7, available from *www.cfr.org/conflict-assessment/preventive-*

priorities-survey-2017/p38562, accessed January 14, 2017; Council on Foreign Affairs, *Global Conflict Tracker*, Washington, DC: Council on Foreign Relations, 2016, available from *www.cfr.org/global/ global-conflict-tracker/p32137#!/*, accessed February 29, 2016; and Michael Lumbers, "Whither the Pivot? Alternative U.S. Strategies for Responding to China's Rise," *Comparative Strategy*, Vol. 34, No. 4, September-October 2015, p. 313, available from *dx.doi.org/1 0.1080/01495933.2015.1069510*, accessed January 23, 2016.

101. Olsen, p. 2.

102. Bickford *et al.*, p. 21.

103. Metz; and Pavgi.

104. Bonin, "Roles and Responsibilities of an Army Service Command Component," slide 2.

105. Enabling competencies are "several vital capabilities . . . [that] are fundamental to the Army's ability to maneuver and secure land areas for the joint force." See HQDA, *The Army*, p. 3-3; and John A. Bonin, Professor of Concepts and Doctrine, Center for Strategic Leadership (CSL), U.S. Army War College, Carlisle Barracks, PA, February 25, 2016, e-mail discussion with the present author; U.S. Naval War College (USNWC), *Joint Military Operations Reference Guide: Forces/Capabilities Handbook*, NWC 3153L, Newport, RI: U.S. Naval War College, July 2011, p. 69, available from *keystone.ndu.edu/Portals/86/Documents/JointMilitaryOperationsReferenceGuide.pdf*, accessed January 13, 2016; and Deni, "Strategic Landpower in the Indo-Asia-Pacific," p. 78.

106. Cunningham, p. 168; Bickford *et al.*, p. 61; HQDA, TRADOC, *The U.S. Army Operating Concept*, p. i.; USNWC, pp. 30, 35; and Department of Defense (DoD), *Functions of the Department of Defense and Its Major Components*, DoD Directive 5100.01, Washington, DC: U.S. Department of Defense, December 21, 2010, p. 30, available from *www.dtic.mil/whs/directives/corres/pdf/510 001p.pdf*, accessed April 10, 2016.

107. HQDA, *The Army*, p. 3-7; and Bonin, e-mail, April 8, 2016.

108. Bickford *et al.*, pp. 65-66; and Deni, *The Future of American Landpower*, p. 10.

109. Freier *et al.*, *U.S. Ground Force Capabilities*, pp. 7, 64; and HQDA, TRADOC, *The U.S. Army Operating Concept*, p. 23.

110. HQDA, *The Army*, p. 1-8; Ray Odierno, "The Force of Tomorrow," *Foreign Policy*, February 4, 2013, available from *foreignpolicy.com/2013/02/04/the-force-of-tomorrow/*, accessed February 2, 2016; Green *et al.*, p. 167; Bickford *et al.*, p. 68; and HQDA, TRADOC, *The U.S. Army Operating Concept*, p. 17.

111. USNWC, pp. 68-69; and USDN, p. 2-31.

112. Bickford *et al.*, pp. 53, 68; HQDA, *Executive Agent Responsibilities Assigned to the Secretary of the Army*, DA Memo 10-1, Washington, DC: U.S. Government Printing Office, January 15, 1997, p. 17; Odierno; Green *et al.*, p. 132; and Bonin, e-mail, February 25, 2016.

113. Bickford *et al.*, pp. 68-69; John A. Bonin, "Doctrine for Joint Land Operations," presentation slides, Center for Strategic Leadership (CSL), U.S. Army War College, Carlisle Barracks, PA, November 2015, slide 8; John A. Bonin, "The Army," presentation slides, Center for Strategic Leadership (CSL), U.S. Army War College, Carlisle Barracks, PA, February 28, 2016, slide 5; and Bonin, e-mail, April 8, 2016.

114. Bonin, "The Army," slide 15.

115. Bonin, "Roles and Responsibilities of an Army Service Command Component," slide 2.

116. Robert W. Cone, *Operationalizing Strategic Landpower*, Fort Eustis, VA: U.S. Commanders Planning Group, Headquarters, Army Training and Doctrine Command, June 27, 2013, p. 8, available from *https://csis.org/files/RUSI%20TRANSCRIPT%20v6%20with%20embedded%20slides.pdf*, accessed January 31, 2016.

117. Core competencies are defined as "indispensable contributions to the joint force." Bonin, "Roles and Responsibilities of an Army Service Command Component," slide 3.

118. Panetta, pp. 4-6.

119. HQDA, TRADOC, *Unified Land Operations*, p. 6.

120. HQDA, *The Army*, p. 3-4.

121. Nathan P. Freier, proj. dir., David Berteau, prog. dir., Stephanie Sanok, Jaquelyn Guy, Curtis Buzzard, Errol Laumann, Steven Nicolucci, J.P. Pellegrino, Sam Eaton, Megan Loney, contrib. auth., *Beyond the Last War: Balancing Ground Forces and Future Challenges Risk in USCENTCOM and USPACOM*, Washington, DC: Center for Strategic and International Studies, April 2013, p. 72, available from *csis.org/files/publication/130424_Freier_Beyond-LastWar_Web.pdf*, accessed February 2, 2016; and Hoffman, p. 9.

122. Freier *et al.*, *U.S. Ground Force Capabilities*, p. vii.

123. Sydney J. Freedberg, Jr., "SASC Pushes Bigger Army Role in Pacific Vs. China," Breaking Defense, May 27, 2015, available from *breakingdefense.com/2015/05/sasc-pushes-bigger-army-role-in-pacific-vs-china/*, accessed February 20, 2016.

124. Joint Chiefs of Staff, JOAC, pp. 31-32.

125. Robert P. Kozloski, "Marching Toward the Sweet Spot: Options for the U.S. Marine Corps in a Time of Austerity," *Naval War College Review*, Vol. 66, No. 3, June 2013, p. 22, available from *https://www.usnwc.edu/getattachment/3e4a9be3-74fe-4bfd-ad8f-7c34b76242fd/Marching-toward-the-Sweet-Spot--Options-for-the-U-.aspx*, accessed January 19, 2016; and USNWC, p. 69.

126. Braun, written comments to the present author, July 15, 2016.

127. USNWC, p. 69; and Parmeter, p. 13.

128. Bonin, e-mail, April 8, 2016.

129. DoD, *Functions of the Department of Defense and Its Major Components*, p. 30.

130. Green *et al.*, pp. 16, 64, 167; Freedberg, Jr., "SASC Pushes Bigger Army Role in Pacific Vs. China"; Freedberg, Jr., "Reshape US Army, Asian Alliances to Deter China"; E. John Teichert, "What Should We Do If the Bomber Can't Get Through?" War on the Rocks, September 16, 2015, available from *warontherocks. com/2015/09/what-should-we-do-if-the-bomber-cant-get-through/*, accessed February 11, 2016; and Lowsen.

131. Jim Thomas, "Why the U.S. Army Needs Missiles: A New Mission to Save the Service," *Foreign Affairs*, Vol. 92, No. 3, May/June 2013, pp. 137-138; Devan Joseph and Amanda Macias, "Meet America's THAAD: One of the world's most advanced missile-defense systems that has China spooked," *Business Insider*, October 18, 2015, available from *www.businessinsider.com/thaad-missile-defense-systems-south-korea-usa-2015-10*, accessed February 9, 2016; Field and Pikner; and Bonin, e-mail, April 8, 2016.

132. Deni, "Strategic Landpower in the Indo-Asia-Pacific," pp. 79-80; HQDA, *The Army*, pp. 3-3; Green *et al.*, pp. 138-139; Joseph and Macias.

133. Deni, "Strategic Landpower in the Indo-Asia-Pacific," p. 80; Armando J. Heredia, "Analysis: New U.S.-Philippine Basing Deal Heavy on Air Power, Light on Naval Support," *USNI News*, March 22, 2016, available from *https://news.usni.org/2016/03/22/analysis-new-u-s-philippine-basing-deal-heavy-on-air-power-light-on-naval-support*, accessed March 29, 2016; and Center for Strategic and International Studies (CSIS), "Terminal High Altitude Air Defense (THAAD)," Missile Threat, CSIS Missile Defense Project, n.d., available from *https://missilethreat.csis.org/system/thaad/*, accessed April 18, 2017.

134. Geoff Fein, "US Army's Patriot missile defence system successfully downs a ballistic missile target," *IHS Jane's Defence Weekly*, March 22, 2016, available from *janes.ihs.com/DefenceWeekly/Display/1765526*, accessed March 28, 2016; and Green *et al.*, pp. 138-139.

135. S. Edward Boxx, and Jason Schuyler, "The Case for the Joint Theater Air Missile Defense Board," *Joint Force Quarterly*, Vol. 79, 4th Qtr., October 2015, p. 84; Teichert; and Deni, "Strategic Landpower in the Indo-Asia-Pacific," p. 80.

136. John A. Bonin, "Landpower ASAP TSC-07," presentation slides, Center for Strategic Leadership (CSL), U.S. Army War College, Carlisle Barracks, PA, March 4, 2016, slide 10; Office of the Secretary of Defense, p. 39; and Green *et al.*, pp. 140, 218.

137. Deni, "Strategic Landpower in the Indo-Asia-Pacific," p. 80; and Freedberg, Jr., "SASC Pushes Bigger Army Role in Pacific Vs. China."

138. Freedberg, Jr., "SASC Pushes Bigger Army Role in Pacific Vs. China."

139. Chamberlain.

140. Peter W. Singer, "From fuzzy to focus: Questions to ask about strategic land power," *Armed Forces Journal*, December 18, 2013, available from *www.armedforcesjournal.com/from-fuzzy-to-focus-questions-to-ask-about-strategic-land-power/*, accessed January 13, 2016; and Harris, Jr.

141. HQDA, TRADOC, *The U.S. Army Operating Concept*, p. 3; Martin E. Dempsey, "Foreword," in Joint Chiefs of Staff, JOAC, Joint Concepts, Washington, DC: U.S. Department of Defense, January 2012, available from *www.dtic.mil/doctrine/concepts/joint_concepts/joac_2012.pdf*, accessed April 13, 2017; Freedberg, Jr., "SASC Pushes Bigger Army Role in Pacific Vs. China"; and Olsen, pp. 6, 44-45.

142. Field and Pikner; and J. Thomas.

143. Olsen, p. 6; and Field and Pikner.

144. J. Thomas; Freedberg, Jr., "Reshape US Army, Asian Alliances to Deter China"; and Sydney J. Freedberg, Jr., "Japan Blazes Trail for US Army: Coastal Defense Vs. China," Breaking Defense, July 15, 2015, available from *breakingdefense.com/2015/07/japan-blazes-trail-for-us-army-coastal-defense-vs-china/*, accessed February 20, 2016.

145. Kris Osborn, "U.S. May Put Weapons in South China Sea," *The National Interest*, January 1, 2017, available from *nationalinterest.org/blog/the-buzz/us-may-put-weapons-south-china-sea-18914*, accessed May 26, 2017.

146. Bickford *et al.*, p. 42; Freedberg, Jr., "Japan Blazes Trail for US Army"; and Teichert.

147. Richard D. Fisher, Jr., "Imagery Suggests China has Deployed YJ-62 Anti-ship Missiles to Woody Island," *IHS Jane's Defence Weekly*, March 23, 2016, available from *janes.ihs.com/Defence-Weekly/Display/1765554*, accessed March 31, 2016.

148. The People's Navy of Vietnam already employs the Russian coastal defense missile system, K-300P Bastion, with a range of 300 km to defend its shores. This system lacks the range to reach much of the Paracels or any of the Spratly Islands, but is estimated to be able to reach China's Shanya Naval Base on Hainan Dao. "Vietnam's K-330P system can attack Chinese targets in Hainan," Defense Blog, available from *http://defence-blog.com/news/vietnams-k-300p-system-can-attack-chinese-targets-in-hainan.html*, accessed April 28, 2017; and Green *et al.*, p. 106.

149. Freedberg, Jr., "What Lessons Do China's Island Bases Offer the US Army."

150. Harris, Jr.

151. Deni, "Strategic Landpower in the Indo-Asia-Pacific," p. 79; and Freedberg, Jr., "Japan Blazes Trail for US Army."

152. HQDA, *The Army*, p. 3-4; and Freedberg, Jr., "SASC Pushes Bigger Army Role in Pacific Vs. China."

153. Freedberg, Jr., "Reshape US Army, Asian Alliances to Deter China"; J. Thomas; and Chamberlain.

154. Freedberg, Jr., "Reshape US Army, Asian Alliances to Deter China"; Jakub Grygiel, "Arming Our Allies: The Case for Offensive Capabilities," *Parameters*, Vol. 45, No. 3, Autumn 2015, p. 48, available from *ssi.armywarcollege.edu/pubs/Parameters/issues/Autumn_2015/Parameters%20Autumn%202015%20Vol45%20No3_ONLINE.pdf*, accessed February 10, 2015; and J. Thomas.

155. J. Thomas; Grygiel; and Freedberg, Jr., "Japan Blazes Trail for US Army."

156. J. Thomas; and Osborn.

157. A 500 km surface-to-surface missile does not exist in the U.S. inventory, so it would need to be acquired for a fully effective counterland mission in the South China Sea. However, 500 km would be the limit set in 1987 by the U.S.-Soviet Intermediate Range Nuclear Forces (INF) Treaty, which required the United States to scrap the Pershing II missile, and which Russia arguably violates today; J. Thomas.

158. Harris, Jr.; and Freedberg, Jr., "What Lessons Do China's Island Bases Offer the US Army."

159. Antulio J. Echevarria, "How Should We Think about 'Gray-Zone' Wars?" *Infinity Journal*, Vol. 5, Iss. 1, Fall 2015, p. 19, available from *https://www.infinityjournal.com/article/158/How_Should_We_Think_about_GrayZone_Wars/*, accessed January 29, 2016.

160. HQDA, TRADOC, *Unified Land Operations*, Foreword and p. 14.

161. Nicholson and Trevithick.

162. Andrew D. Preston, *The Asia Pacific Rebalance: Tipping the Scale with Landpower*, Civilian Research Project, Carlisle Barracks, PA: U.S. Army War College, April 2013, available from *www.dtic.mil/cgi-bin/GetTRDoc?AD=ADA592975*, accessed June 13, 2016.

163. Both the Marine Corps and Army are assigned the functions of amphibious warfare, and the Army is also assigned the functions of airborne and air assault. DoD, *Functions of the Department of Defense and Its Major Components*, pp. 30, 32; USDN, p. 1-16; and HQDA, TRADOC, *The U.S. Army Operating Concept*, p. 23.

164. Kozloski, p. 19; and Olsen, p. 51.

165. Shenberger, pp. 16-17.

166. Michael F. Perry, *Importance of Seabasing to Land Power Generation*, Program Research Project, Carlisle Barracks: U.S. Army War College, May 2009, pp. 2, 15, available from *www.dtic.mil/docs/citations/ADA508337*, accessed February 8, 2016; Shenberger, pp. 14-15; and Joseph R. Corleto, *Future Joint Seabasing in*

the Asia-Pacific Region, Strategy Research Project, Carlisle Barracks, PA: U.S. Army War College, 2013, pp. 7-8, available from *www.dtic.mil/docs/citations/ADA553114*, accessed Februrary 8, 2016.

167. USDN, pp. 2-22-2-24; Perry, p. 16; Shenberger, p. 21; and Corleto, p. 25.

168. Perry, pp. 13-14; Green *et al.*, p. 134; and Corleto, pp. 8, 25.

169. Joe Gould, "US Army To Choose New Landing Craft Next Year," DefenseNews.com, August 26, 2015, available from *www.defensenews.com/story/defense/2015/08/26/us-army-choose-new-landing-craft-next-year/32424371/*, accessed February 10, 2015; and Grace Jean, "US Army helicopters to continue training with US Navy ships," *IHS Jane's Defence Weekly*, December 8, 2015, available from *janes.ihs.com/DefenceWeekly/Display/1758226*, accessed February 7, 2015.

170. HQDA, TRADOC, *The U.S. Army Operating Concept*, p. 23; and Office of the Secretary of Defense, pp. 36-37.

171. HQDA, *The Army*, pp. 3-2, 3-5; Nicholson and Trevithick; Bickford *et al.*, pp. 26-27; and Joint Chiefs of Staff, JOAC, pp. 22, 30.

172. Freedberg, Jr., "What Lessons Do China's Island Bases Offer the US Army."

173. USNWC, pp. 82-83; and Nicholson and Trevithick.

174. Grygiel, pp. 39-40.

175. The first island chain that China considers hemming it in stretches from Japan to Taiwan, the Philippines and Borneo, and the second island chain, in the mid-Pacific Ocean, goes from the Ogasawara and Volcano Islands to the U.S. Marianas and Guam. Gadd, p. 9; Green *et al.*, p. 4; and Gregory B. Poling, "Rationalizing U.S. Goals in the South China Sea," *Journal of Political Risk*, Vol. 3, No. 9, September 2015, available from *www.jpolrisk.com/rationalizing-u-s-goals-in-the-south-china-sea/*, accessed January 26, 2016.

176. Freier *et al.*, *U.S. Ground Force Capabilities*, p. 52; Bickford *et al.*, p. 53; Olsen, pp. 51-52; and Shenberger, p. 22.

177. Shenberger, pp. 2-3, 22; Green *et al.*, p. 132; Corleto, p. 2; Ryan Faith, "Can the US Army Still Fight as a Heavyweight?" Vice News, August 4, 2015, available from *https://news.vice.com/article/can-the-us-army-still-fight-as-a-heavyweight*, accessed February 5, 2016; and Perry, p. 16.

178. Shenberger, p. 17; and Freedberg, Jr., "Japan Blazes Trail for US Army."

179. Echevarria, p. 18; and USDN, pp. 4-2-4-3.

180. USDN, p. 1-11.

181. HQDA, *The Army*, p. 1-5; Katrosh, p. 28; Panetta, p. 8; Nicholas R. Krueger, "The Rationale for a Robust U.S. Army Presence in the Pacific Basin," *National Security Watch*, Vol. 12-2, March 8, 2012, p. 4, available from *https://www.ausa.org/file/1586/download?token=O-95HCQu*, accessed April 18, 2017; and Knych.

182. Odierno; Joint Chiefs of Staff, JOAC, p. 3; and USARPAC, *Partnering in the Pacific*, p. 5.

183. Chamberlain.

184. USARPAC, *Partnering in the Pacific*, p. 11; and Echevarria, p. 17.

185. Green *et al.*, p. 13; Barno, Bensahel, and Sharp, p. 165; and Robert H. Scales and Larry M. Wortzel, *The Future U.S. Military Presence in Asia: Landpower and the Geostrategy of American Commitment*, Carlisle, PA: Strategic Studies Institute, U.S. Army War College, April 1, 1999, p. 1, available from *ssi.armywarcollege.edu/pubs/display.cfm?pubID=75*, accessed April 18, 2017.

186. Leonard A. Housley, *Multinational Training Opportunities in the Asia-Pacific*, Strategy Research Project, Carlisle Barracks, PA: U.S. Army War College, 2013, p. 11, available from *handle.dtic.mil/100.2/ADA589344*, accessed March 15, 2016; Green *et al.*, p. 34; and Deni, *The Future of American Landpower*, pp. 34-35, 38-39.

187. Olsen, p. 50; Trefor Moss, "U.S., Philippines Forge Closer Military Ties Amid China Tensions," *The Wall Street Journal*, October 8, 2015, available from *www.wsj.com/article_email/u-s-philippines-forge-closer-military-ties-amid-china-tensions-1444304011-lMyQjAxMTA1OTA1OTQwNTk0Wj*, accessed February 17, 2016.

188. Teichert; Field and Pikner; Office of the Secretary of Defense, p. 16; and Seth Robson, "US Buildup in Philippines Raises Stakes in Region," *Stars and Stripes*, February 3, 2016, available from *https://www.stripes.com/news/us-buildup-in-philippines-raises-stakes-in-region-1.391912#.WPdT4EdMRpg*, accessed February 6, 2016.

189. Deni, *The Future of American Landpower*, pp. 27-28; Green *et al.*, p. 77; Poling; and Stokes, p. 17.

190. Scales and Wortzel, p. 5; and Green *et al.*, p. 32.

191. Joint Chiefs of Staff, JOAC, p. 7.

192. Panetta, pp. 4-6; Fernando M. Luján, *Light Footprints: The Future of American Military Intervention*, Washington, DC: Center for a New American Security, March 2013, p. 5, available from *https://www.cnas.org/publications/reports/light-footprints-the-future-of-american-military-intervention*, accessed February 15, 2016; Freedberg, Jr., "Reshape US Army, Asian Alliances to Deter China"; and Teichert.

193. Office of the Secretary of Defense, p. viii; Scales and Wortzel, p. 4; Deni, "Strategic Landpower in the Indo-Asia-Pacific," p. 83; Derek Chollet and Julianne Smith, "America's Allies Want More from the US," Defense One, August 3, 2015, available from *www.defenseone.com/ideas/2015/08/americas-allies-want-more-us/118811/*, accessed February 14, 2016; and Green *et al.*, p. 50.

194. Joint Chiefs of Staff, JOAC, p. 20; and Chamberlain.

195. De Swielande, p. 80; and Green *et al.*, pp. 40-41; DoD, *U.S. Asia-Pacific Maritime Security Strategy*, Washington, DC: U.S. Department of Defense, 2015, p. 23, available from *https://admin.govexec.com/media/gbc/docs/pdfs_edit/dod-asia-pacific-maritime-security-strategy.pdf*, accessed January 26, 2016.

196. Thomas G. Mahnken, Dan Blumenthal, Thomas Donnel-ly, Michael Mazza, Gary J. Schmitt, and Andrew Shearer, *Asia in the Balance: Transforming US Military Strategy in Asia*, Washington, DC: American Enterprise Institute, June 2012, p. 15; Joint Chiefs of Staff, JOAC, p. 8; and Bickford *et al.*, pp. 70-71.

197. U.S. Army forces were stationed in Darwin during World War II. Barno, Bensahel, and Sharp, pp. 158-159; Deni, *The Future of American Landpower*, pp. x, 16; and Riccoh Player, *Strategic Pivot Toward the Asia-Pacific: Implications for the USMC*, Strategy Research Project, Carlisle Barracks, PA: U.S. Army War College, March 2013, p. 10, available from *www.dtic.mil/cgi-bin/ GetTRDoc?AD=ADA589881*, accessed January 19, 2016.

198. Scales and Wortzel, p. iii; and Bickford *et al.*, p. v.

199. Parts of the five military installations to house American forces are: Antonio Bautista Air Base (AB), Basa AB, Fort Magsay-say, Lumbia AB, and Mactan-Benito Ebuen AB, along with fur-ther requests for access to Clark International Airport and Camp Aguinaldo, the Philippine Marine Corps' headquarters. Dan Lamonthe, "These are the bases the U.S. will use near the South China Sea. China isn't impressed," *The Washington Post*, March 21, 2016, available from *https://www.washingtonpost.com/news/ checkpoint/wp/2016/03/21/these-are-the-new-u-s-military-bases-near-the-south-china-sea-china-isnt-impressed/?utm_term=.3ea5ff8e0833*, accessed April 17, 2016; Lolita C. Baldor, Associated Press, "U.S. sending commandos, combat aircraft to Philippines," *Navy Times*, April 14, 2016, available from *https://www.navytimes.com/story/ military/2016/04/14/us-reveals-joint-patrols-south-china-sea-philip-pines/83020786/*, accessed April 17, 2016; and Tara Copp, "US to rotate more aircraft, troops through Philippines," *Stars and Stripes*, April 14, 2016, available from *www.stripes.com/news/pacific/us-to-rotate-more-aircraft-troops-through-philippines-1.404418*, accessed April 17, 2016.

200. Green *et al.*, p. 17; and Mark S. Miller, *Maintaining Peace in the South China Sea and the Spratly Islands: Are There Acceptable Alternatives to the U.S. Naval Forces Forward Deployed in the Asia Pacific Region?* Strategy Research Project, Carlisle Barracks, PA: U.S. Army War College, 2002, p. 13, available from *www.dtic.mil/ get-tr-doc/pdf?AD=ADA401689*, accessed February 11, 2016.

201. Mahnken *et al.*, pp. 1, 5; and Shenberger, p. 11.

202. Joint Chiefs of Staff, JOAC, pp. 18-19; and Green *et al.*, p. 164.

203. Bickford *et al.*, p. vi; Housley, pp. 21-22; and Joe Gould, "US Army to Expand Prepositioned Stocks," DefenseNews.com, June 3, 2015, available from *www.defensenews.com/story/defense/land/army/2015/06/03/us-army-aims-to-expand-prepositioned-stocks-africa-asia-pacific-latin-america/28423437/*, accessed February 12, 2016.

204. Bickford *et al.*, pp. 28-29.

205. For example, a light infantry brigade of 3,800 soldiers and 7,300 tons of gear requires 150 C-17 cargo planes and about 5 days to deploy, see Faith; Franz-Stefan Gady, "Deterring China: US Army to Stockpile Equipment in Cambodia and Vietnam," Asia Defense, blog of *The Diplomat*, March 18, 2016, available from *thediplomat.com/2016/03/deterring-china-us-army-to-stockpile-equipment-in-cambodia-and-vietnam/*, accessed April 19, 2016; Gould, "US Army to Expand Prepositioned Stocks"; Green *et al.*, p. 164; and Bickford *et al.*, p. 29.

206. USNWC, pp. 59-60.

207. Excess material could instead be used to fill some prepositioned stocks to reduce the cost involved. Aaron Mehta, "Pentagon Eyeing More Prepositioning of Gear," DefenseNews.com, December 21, 2015, available from *www.defensenews.com/story/defense/policy-budget/policy/2015/12/21/pentagon-expects-more-prepositioning-gear-europe-russia/77700432/*, accessed February 12, 2016.

208. USARPAC, *Partnering in the Pacific*, p. 23; Mehta; and USNWC, p. 59.

209. Green *et al.*, pp. 50, 170; and Mehta.

210. Philippine President Duterte has accused the United States of storing weapons at some of these sites contravening the Enhanced Defense Cooperation Agreement (EDCA)—a charge the American Ambassador has refuted and Philippine military officials have subsequently found baseless. Neil Jerome Morales, rpt.,

Manuel Mogato, auth., and Martin Petty, ed., "U.S. envoy says no American weapons buildup in Philippines," Reuters, January 31, 2017, available from *www.reuters.com/article/us-philippines-usa-idUSKBN15F0MI*, accessed April 19, 2017; Green *et al.*, p. 77; and Agence France-Presse, "Official: Philippines to Offer the Use of Eight Bases to US Forces," DefenseNews.com, January 13, 2016, available from *www.defensenews.com/story/defense/2016/01/13/official-philippines-offer-use-eight-bases-us-forces/78736552/*, accessed February 17, 2017.

211. Sydney J. Freedberg, Jr., "US Army Plans Stockpiles in Vietnam, Cambodia: Hello China," Breaking Defense, March 15, 2016, available from *breakingdefense.com/2016/03/us-army-plans-stockpiles-in-vietnam-cambodia-hello-china/*, accessed April 18, 2017; Gady, "Deterring China"; Gould, "US Army to Expand Prepositioned Stocks"; and Bickford *et al.*, p. 29.

212. Gady, "Deterring China."

213. Mehta.

214. Freedberg, Jr., "US Army Plans Stockpiles in Vietnam, Cambodia."

215. Green *et al.*, p. 164; and USDN, p. 2-30.

216. Bonin, "Landpower ASAP TSC-07," slide 49; and USDN, p. 5-4.

217. USDN, p. 5-2.

218. Ann E. Stafford, former Associate Dean, Joint Forces Staff College, Norfolk, VA, e-mail discussion with the present author, April 23, 2016.

219. Panetta, pp. 4-6; De Swielande, p. 86; Bickford *et al.*, pp. iv, 23, 54; and Jeong Lee, "On 'Strategic Landpower in the Indo-Asia-Pacific'," *Parameters*, Vol. 43, No. 4, Winter 2013-14, pp. 128-130, available from *http://ssi.armywarcollege.edu/pubs/Parameters/Issues/Winter_2013/TheQuarterly_Winter2013-14_v43n4.pdf*, accessed April 28, 2017.

220. Pierce, Douds, and Marra, pp. 58-59.

221. De Swielande, p. 86; USDN, pp. 2-16, 4-4-4-6; Nicholson and Trevithick; Player, p. 17; and Joint Chiefs of Staff, *Special Operations*, p. II-11.

222. Joint Chiefs of Staff, *Special Operations*, pp. x-xii, I-9; and Office of the Secretary of Defense, p. 37.

223. "Joint Special Operations Task Force—Philippines (JSOTF-P)," GlobalSecurity.org, last modified October 8, 2013, available from *www.globalsecurity.org/military/agency/dod/jsotf-p. htm*, accessed April 21, 2016; and Bickford *et al.*, p. 54.

224. Per Liljas, "ISIS Is Making Inroads in the Southern Philippines and the Implications for Asia Are Alarming," *Time*, April 14, 2016, available from *time.com/4293395/isis-zamboanga-mind-anao-moro-islamist-terrorist-asia-philippines-abu-sayyaf/*, accessed April 23, 2016.

225. Freier *et al.*, *Beyond the Last War*, p. 41.

226. Takashi Kawamoto and Yizhe Daniel Xie, "An HA/DR Solution to South China Sea Tensions," Flashpoints, blog of *The Diplomat*, July 18, 2015, available from *thediplomat.com/2015/07/an-hadr-solution-to-south-china-sea-tensions/*, accessed December 30, 2015.

227. Panetta, pp. 4-6; Freier *et al.*, *U.S. Ground Force Capabilities*, p. 26; Parmeter, pp. 12-13; and HQDA, *The Army*, pp. 3-2-3-3.

228. USDN, p. 5-4; and Joint Chiefs of Staff, *Special Operations*, p. I-14.

229. Joint Chiefs of Staff, *Civil-Military Operations*, JP 3-57, Washington, DC: U.S. Department of Defense, September 11, 2013, p. II-5, available from *www.dtic.mil/doctrine/new_pubs/jp3_57. pdf*, accessed April 24, 2016; Bickford *et al.*, pp. 68-69; and Joint Chiefs of Staff, *Special Operations*, p. I-14.

230. USDN, p. 5-4; Bickford *et al.*, pp. 21-22; Mike Ellicott, "The Army Engineer Regiment and the Future," in Samuel R.

White, Jr., ed., *Futures Seminar: the United States Army in 2025 and Beyond*, Vol. 2, Carlisle Barracks, PA: Center for Strategic Leadership, U.S. Army War College, December 2015, pp. 78-79, available from *https://csl.armywarcollege.edu/usacsl/publications/ FuturesElectiveCompendium(Vol%202%20-%202015).pdf*, accessed January 15, 2016; and Deni, "Strategic Landpower in the Indo-Asia-Pacific," p. 79.

231. Thomas Lum and Rhoda Margesson, *Typhoon Haiyan (Yolanda): U.S. and International Response to Philippines Disaster*, Report No. R43309, Washington, DC: U.S. Library of Congress, Congressional Research Service, February 10, 2014, Summary, available from *https://www.fas.org/sgp/crs/row/R43309.pdf*, accessed April 25, 2016; and Office of the Press Secretary, "Fact Sheet: U.S. Response to Typhoon Haiyan," Washington, DC: The White House, November 19, 2013, available from *https://obamawhite-house.archives.gov/the-press-office/2013/11/19/fact-sheet-us-response-typhoon-haiyan*, accessed April 25, 2016.

232. Andrew Feickert and Emma Chanlett-Avery, *Japan 2011 Earthquake: U.S. Department of Defense (DoD) Response*, Report No. R41690, Washington, DC: U.S. Library of Congress, Congressional Research Service, June 2, 2011, Summary, available from *https://www.hsdl.org/?view&did=4139*, accessed April 26, 2017; Jeff Schogol, "U.S. military steps up Japan earthquake relief mission," *Marine Corps Times*, April 18, 2016, available from *https://www. marinecorpstimes.com/story/military/2016/04/18/us-steps-up-japan-earthquake-relief-mission/83187580/*, accessed April 25, 2016; Green *et al.*, p. 42; and USARPAC, *Partnering in the Pacific*, p. 3.

233. Office of the Press Secretary; Freier *et al.*, *Beyond the Last War*, pp. 48-49; and Green *et al.*, p. 170.

234. Freier *et al.*, *Beyond the Last War*, p. 49.

235. Metz.

236. "Influence, Engagement, and Shape" helps to "maximize combat power " as the U.S. Army's seventh Warfighting Function, listed with other critical functions such as movement and maneuver, fires, intelligence, protection, sustainment, and mission command. Martin; Odierno, Amos, and McRaven, p. 8; Freier *et al.*, *Beyond the Last War*, pp. 72-73; and HQDA, *The Army*, pp. 1-1-1-2.

237. Harris, Jr.; Odierno, Amos, and McRaven, p. 5; and Bickford *et al.*, p. 70.

238. Joint Chiefs of Staff, JOAC, pp. i, 18; and Michelle Tan, "Army seeks partnerships, new technology in the Pacific," *Army Times*, October 19, 2015, available from *www.armytimes.com/story/ military/careers/army/2015/10/19/army-seeks-partnerships-new-tech-nology-pacific/73299074/*, accessed January 27, 2016.

239. Bonin, "Landpower ASAP TSC-07," slides 48-49.

240. Odierno, Amos, and McRaven, pp. 3-4; USDN, p. 4-2; Bickford *et al.*, p. 18; USARPAC, *Partnering in the Pacific*, p. 3; and H.R. McMaster, "Continuity and Change: The Army Operating Concept and Clear Thinking About Future War," *Military Review*, Vol. 95, No. 2, March-April 2015, p. 14, available from *www.ncfa. ncr.gov/sites/default/files/2%20McMaster_Continuity%20and%20 Change_The%20Army%20Operating%20Concept%20and%20 Clear%20Thinking%20About%20Future%20War.pdf*, accessed January 12, 2015.

241. USARPAC, *Partnering in the Pacific*, p. 6; USDN, p. 4-1; and Joint Chiefs of Staff, *Special Operations*, p. I-8.

242. Bickford *et al.*, p. 18; and Arthur Chi Wing Fong, *Dancing with the Dragon: U.S.-China Engagement Policy*, Strategy Research Project, Carlisle Barracks, PA: U.S. Army War College, 2013, pp. 11-12, available from *www.dtic.mil/cgi-bin/ GetTRDoc?AD=ADA589225*, accessed February 19, 2016.

243. Joint Chiefs of Staff, JOAC, p. 18; HQDA, *The Army*, p. 1-5; and Freier *et al.*, *Beyond the Last War*, p. 44.

244. Bickford *et al.*, p. 17; and USARPAC, *Partnering in the Pacific*, p. 4.

245. Robert M. Gates, "Helping Others Defend Themselves: The Future of U.S. Security Assistance," *Foreign Affairs*, Vol. 89, No. 3, May/June 2010, p. 2; Singer; and Green *et al.*, p. 9.

246. Grant Newsham, "'Amphibiosity' in the Asia-Pacific," *Proceedings: United States Naval Institute*, Vol. 141, No. 11, Novem-

ber 2015; Peter Lichtenbaum, John G. McGinn, Matt Breen, and Adam Cushing, "Improving Security Cooperation: A Win-Win," War on the Rocks, July 7, 2015, available from *warontherocks. com/2015/07/improving-security-cooperation-a-win-win/*, accessed February 15, 2016; Bickford *et al.*, p. 36; and USARPAC, *Partnering in the Pacific*, p. 3.

247. Bickford *et al.*, p. vii; Odierno, Amos, and McRaven, p. 6; Olsen, p. 53; and USARPAC, *Partnering in the Pacific*, p. 1.

248. Amber Corrin, "Interoperability: The key to Army readiness," C4ISRNET, March 17, 2016, available from *www. c4isrnet.com/story/military-tech/show-reporter/global-force-sympo- sium/2016/03/17/interoperability-key-army-readiness/81908934/*, ac- cessed April 30, 2016; Housley, p. 8; Green *et al.*, p. 10; Newsham; Freier *et al.*, *Beyond the Last War*, p. 44; and Teichert.

249. Housley, p. 8; and Teichert.

250. Rapp-Hooper; and Desmond Walton, "A Reinvigorated Strategic Alliance," The Cipher Brief, April 15, 2016, available from *thecipherbrief.com/article/asia/reinvigorated-strategic-alliance-1093*, accessed April 17, 2016.

251. Bickford *et al.*, pp. 68-69; Deni, "Strategic Landpower in the Indo-Asia-Pacific," p. 82; Odierno, Amos, and McRaven, p. 6; Olsen, p. 50; and Green *et al.*, p. 29.

252. Odierno, Amos, and McRaven, pp. 17-18; USARPAC, *Partnering in the Pacific*, pp. 5-6; and HQDA, TRADOC, *The U.S. Army Operating Concept*, p. 22.

253. Freedberg, Jr., "After '10 Years of Abject Failure'"; and Luján, p. 16.

254. Newsham.

255. Jack Midgley, "Building Partner Capability: Defining an Army Role in Future Small Wars," *Small Wars Journal*, Vol. 8, No. 2, February 20, 2012, available from *www.smallwarsjournal. com/jrnl/art/building-partner-capability*, accessed February 2, 2016; HQDA, TRADOC, *The U.S. Army Operating Concept*, pp. 17, 22; and Green *et al.*, p. 135.

256. Olsen, pp. 50-51; USARPAC, *Partnering in the Pacific*, p. 3; USDN, p. 1-16; U.S. Army SOCOM, p. 22; HQDA, TRADOC, *The U.S. Army Operating Concept*, p. 22; Bickford *et al.*, *The Role of the U.S. Army in Asia*, p. 43.

257. Bickford *et al.*, pp. 18-19.

258. Joint Chiefs of Staff, *DOD Dictionary of Military and Associated Terms*, p. 210.

259. USDN, p. 4-2; Green *et al.*, p. 173; and Deni, "Strategic Landpower in the Indo-Asia-Pacific," p. 81.

260. Deni, "Strategic Landpower in the Indo-Asia-Pacific," pp. 81-82; and Housley, p. 9.

261. Green *et al.*, p. 171.

262. Freier *et al.*, *Beyond the Last War*, p. 43; Joint Chiefs of Staff, JOAC, p. 19; and HQDA, *The Army*, p. 3-4.

263. HQDA, *The Army*, p. 3-5.

264. Deni, *The Future of American Landpower*, p. 3; Housley, p. 13; Joint Chiefs of Staff, JOAC, pp. 18-19; Stokes, p. 15; and USARPAC, *Partnering in the Pacific*, p. 23.

265. Joint Chiefs of Staff, *DOD Dictionary of Military and Associated Terms*, p. 210.

266. Jen Judson, "Brooks: Pacific Pathways Generating Savings, Highlighting Challenges," DefenseNews.com, December 8, 2015, available from *www.defensenews.com/story/defense/land/army/2015/12/08/brooks-pacific-pathways-generating-savings-highlighting-challenges/76982200/*, accessed January 31, 2016; and Daniel Gouré, "Foreign Military Sales Remain an Important Tool of U.S. National Security," Lexington Institute, February 26, 2016, available from *lexingtoninstitute.org/foreign-military-sales-remain-an-important-tool-of-u-s-national-security/*, accessed May 5, 2016.

267. Jen Judson, "Army's Annual Foreign Military Sales Top $20 Billion," DefenseNews.com, October 13, 2015, available from

www.defensenews.com/story/defense/show-daily/ausa/2015/10/13/ar-my-conducts-thriving-business-abroad/73874016/, accessed February 16, 2016.

268. Stokes, p. 17; Bickford *et al.*, p. 73.

269. Bickford *et al.*, pp. v, vii; and Stokes, p. 17.

270. Michelle Tan, "Here's how the Army's pacific mission is expanding now," *Army Times*, May 14, 2016, available from *www.armytimes.com/story/military/2016/05/14/heres-how-armys-pacific-mission-expanding-now/84241910/*, accessed May 16, 2016; Tan, "Army seeks partnerships, new technology in the Pacific"; Judson, "Brooks"; William G. Braun III and David Lai, eds., *U.S.-China Competition: Asia-Pacific Land Force Implications, A U.S. Army War College Integrated Research Project in Support of U.S. Army Pacific Command and Headquarters, Department of the Army, Directorate of Strategy and Policy (HQDA G-35)*, Carlisle, PA: Strategic Studies Institute, U.S. Army War College, November 2016, p. 47, available from *ssi.armywarcollege.edu/pubs/display.cfm?pubID=1333*, accessed January 22, 2017; and Richard Sisk, "US Army Wants Permanent Missile Defense System on Guam," Military.com, December 8, 2015, available from *www.military.com/daily-news/2015/12/08/us-army-wants-permanent-missile-defense-system-on-guam.html*, accessed February 15, 2016.

271. Wikipedia contributors, "Cobra Gold," Wikipedia, the free encyclopedia, February 17, 2016, available from *https://en.wikipedia.org/w/index.php?title=Cobra_Gold&oldid=705463829*, accessed May 9, 2016; and Stephen C. Myers, *Military Cooperation Frameworks: Effective Models to Address Transnational Security Challenges of the Asia-Pacific Region*, Civilian Research Project, Carlisle Barracks, PA: U.S. Army War College, 2011, p. 20, available from *www.dtic.mil/dtic/tr/fulltext/u2/a565132.pdf*, accessed February 16, 2016.

272. U.S. Third Fleet Public Affairs, "27 Nations to Participate in World's Largest Maritime Exercise," U.S. Pacific Command, June 1, 2016, available from *www.pacom.mil/Media/News/News-ArticleView/tabid/11348/Article/788436/27-nations-to-participate-in-worlds-largest-maritime-exercise.aspx*, accessed June 10, 2016; June Teufel Dreyer, "Washington Contemplates the Chinese Military,"

E-Notes, Foreign Policy Research Institute, September 1, 2015, available from *www.fpri.org/article/2015/09/washington-contemplates-the-chinese-military/*, accessed on April 19, 2017.

273. Deni, *The Future of American Landpower*, p. 40; Green *et al.*, pp. 12, 132; and Newsham.

274. USARPAC, *Partnering in the Pacific*, p. 3; Parmeter, p. 14; and Bickford *et al.*, pp. 71-72.

275. Miller, pp. 13-14.

276. USPACOM Public Affairs Office, "Foreign Military Leaders Observe U.S. Marine Corps Amphibious Landing during U.S. Pacific Command Amphibious Leaders Symposium," U.S. Pacific Command, May 20, 2015, available from *www.pacom.mil/Media/News/tabid/5693/Article/589347/foreign-military-leaders-observe-us-marine-corps-amphibious-landing-during-us-p.aspx*, accessed May 16, 2016; Newsham; Green *et al.*, p. 132; and Harley Thomas, "PALS-15 Unites Pacific," Official U.S. Marine Corps Website, May 22, 2015, available from *www.marines.mil/News/NewsDisplay/tabid/3258/Article/589525/pals-15-unites-pacific.aspx*, accessed May 10, 2016.

277. Stokes, p. 17; and Robert Johnson, "Why the US Appointing an Aussie General to Command Its Pacific Troops is a Big Deal," *Business Insider*, February 2, 2013, available from *www.businessinsider.com/usarpac-post-australian-major-general-richard-burr-australian-defence-force-2013-2*, accessed May 9, 2016.

278. Newsham.

279. The Marine Corps does not regionally align its forces, while SOF forces do. Deni, *The Future of American Landpower*, p. 14; Deni, "Strategic Landpower in the Indo-Asia-Pacific," pp. 82-83; Green *et al.*, pp. 132, 135; and Bickford *et al.*, pp. 72-73.

280. Field and Pikner.

281. Joint Chiefs of Staff, *DOD Dictionary of Military and Associated Terms*, p. 210.

282. Green *et al.*, p. 105; and Bickford *et al.*, p. 40.

283. Yevgen Sautin, "This Vietnamese Base Will Decide the South China Sea's Fate," *The National Interest*, May 8, 2016, available from *nationalinterest.org/feature/vietnamese-base-will-decide-the-south-china-seas-fate-16093?page=2*, accessed May 10, 2016.

284. USARPAC, *Partnering in the Pacific*, p. 8.

285. Alexander L. Vuving, "A Tipping Point in the US-China-Vietnam Triangle," Features, online news articles of *The Diplomat*, July 6, 2015, available from *thediplomat.com/2015/07/a-tipping-point-in-the-u-s-china-vietnam-triangle/*, accessed February 17, 2016; Abraham Muñoz, *Revisiting U.S.-Vietnam Relations Amid the Rebalance to the Pacific*, Strategy Research Project, Carlisle Barracks, PA: U.S. Army War College, 2013, p. 6, available from *www.dtic.mil/dtic/tr/fulltext/u2/a589271.pdf*, accessed February 17, 2016; and Green *et al.*, p. 107.

286. Eric Tegler, "The Practicalities of US Military Sales to Vietnam," Features, online news articles of *The Diplomat*, August 5, 2015, available from *thediplomat.com/2015/08/the-practicalities-of-us-military-sales-to-vietnam/*, accessed February 17, 2016; Muñoz, p. 10; and Richard Weitz, "Vietnam: America's Big Strategic Opportunity in Asia (Think China)," *The National Interest*, May 29, 2016, available from *nationalinterest.org/blog/the-buzz/vietnam-americas-strategic-opportunity-asia-16373?page=2*, accessed June 12, 2016.

287. Freier *et al.*, *Beyond the Last War*, p. 44; De Swielande, p. 82; and Green *et al.*, p. 173.

288. Muñoz, pp. 7-8.

289. Figure sourced from USARPAC, *Partnering in the Pacific*, p. 6.

290. Bickford *et al.*, pp. 41-42.

291. "State Partnership program expands to include Vietnam," *Oregon Sentinel*, Vol. 10, No. 5, Winter 2012, pp. 1, 4, available from *www.oregon.gov/OMD/AGPA/Documents/Winter%20 2012-WEB.pdf*, accessed May 11, 2016; and Nick Choy, "Vietnam

delegation visits Oregon National Guard for State Partnership Program workshop," Salem, OR: Oregon National Guard Public Affairs Office, April 2014, available from *https://www.dvidshub.net/ news/105326/vietnam-delegation-visits-oregon-national-guard-state-partnership-program-workshop#.VzNZwiFKYYA*, accessed May 11, 2016.

292. Muñoz, pp. 6-7; Green *et al.*, p. 107; and David Larter, "Changing times in Vietnam: 5 things troops need to know," *Navy Times*, May 28, 2016, available from *www.navytimes.com/story/military/2016/05/28/vietnam-pacom-port-visits-obama-harris/84848028/*, accessed May 31, 2016.

293. Green *et al.*, pp. 107-108; and Richard Sisk, "US Army Seeks to Expand Role in Asia-Pacific Region, General Says," DOD Buzz, May 25, 2016, available from *www.dodbuzz.com/2016/05/25/ us-vietnam-joint-military-exercises-possible-army-general-says/*, accessed May 30, 2016.

294. Newsham.

295. Freedberg, Jr., "US Army Plans Stockpiles in Vietnam, Cambodia."

296. De Swielande, p. 82; Sautin; and Muñoz, p. 7.

297. Muñoz, p. 7; and Sautin.

298. Sautin; Green *et al.*, p. 107; Harsh V. Pant, "New Equations in the Asia-Pacific as China Arrives as Military Power," China Power, blog of *The Diplomat*, September 21, 2015, available from *thediplomat.com/2015/09/new-equations-in-the-asia-pacific-as-china-arrives-as-military-power/*, accessed February 15, 2016; and "Obama lifts US embargo on lethal arms sales to Vietnam," BBC News, May 23, 2016, available from *www.bbc.com/news/world-asia-36356695*, accessed May 23, 2016.

299. Weitz.

300. David Brunnstrom, Lesley Wroughton, and Matt Spetalnick, "Obama weighs historic decision on whether to lift Vietnam arms ban," Reuters, May 10, 2016 available from *in.reuters.com/*

article/usa-vietnam-embargo-idINKCN0Y02ES, accessed April 19, 2017; Muñoz, p. 9; Green *et al.*, p. 106; and Tegler.

301. Poling.

302. "Malaysia faces tricky Sino-US balancing act," *The Straits Times*, November 6, 2015, available from *www.straitstimes.com/ asia/se-asia/malaysia-faces-tricky-sino-us-balancing-act*, accessed February 17, 2016; Green *et al.*, p. 96; and Zachary Keck, "Malaysia to Establish Marine Corps and South China Sea Naval Base," Flash-points, blog of *The Diplomat*, October 19, 2013, available from *the-diplomat.com/2013/10/malaysia-to-establish-marine-corps-and-south-china-sea-naval-base/*, accessed May 14, 2016.

303. USARPAC, *Partnering in the Pacific*, p. 7.

304. Green *et al.*, pp. 96, 172-173.

305. Prashanth Parameswaran, "US, Brunei Mull New Military Partnership," Rebalance (renamed Trans-Pacific View), blog of *The Diplomat*, March 15, 2016, available from *thediplomat.com/2016/03/us-brunei-mull-new-military-partner ship/*, accessed May 14, 2016. Although receiving briefings on the State Partnership Program (SPP), neither Malaysia nor Brunei has advanced far in joining.

306. Green *et al.*, p. 95; Keck; and Wikipedia contributors, "Malaysian Army," Wikipedia, the free encyclopedia, March 4, 2016, available from *https://en.wikipedia.org/w/index.php?title=Malaysian_ Army&oldid=708230049*, accessed May 15, 2016.

307. Newsham; Joshua Stewart, "Marine Corps Works to Build New Ties in Southeast Asia," *Marine Corps Times*, April 1, 2015; and Emmanuel Ramos, "U.S. Marines, Malaysian Soldiers Complete MALUS AMPHEX 15," Official U.S. Marine Corps Website, November 23, 2015, available from *www.marines.mil/ News/NewsDisplay/tabid/3258/Article/630890/us-marines-malaysian-soldiers-complete-malus-amphex-15.aspx*, accessed May 14, 2015.

308. Stewart, "Marine Corps Works to Build New Ties in Southeast Asia."

309. Brian Erickson, "Opening Ceremony Marks Beginning of Keris Strike 2015," U.S. Pacific Command, September 16, 2015, available from *www.pacom.mil/Media/News/tabid/5693/Article/617463/opening-ceremony-marks-beginning-of-keris-strike-2015.aspx*, accessed May 15, 2016; and Michael McMillan and Brian W. Tuttle, "Logistics for Pacific Pathways: Malaysia," *Army Sustainment*, March-April 2015, p. 42, available from *www.alu.army.mil/alog/2015/MarApr15/PDF/143253.pdf*, accessed June 10, 2016.

310. De Swielande, p. 82; and Reuters, Agence France-Presse, "Malaysia faces tricky Sino-US balancing act."

311. Jon Grevatt, "Malaysian Army Orders MD 530G Helicopters," IHS Jane's 360, February 2, 2016; Franz-Stefan Gady, "Biggest US-Malaysia Arms Deal in 20 Years: Kuala Lumpur to Receive New Attack Helicopters," Asia Defense, blog of *The Diplomat*, February 2, 2016, available from *thediplomat.com/2016/02/biggest-us-malaysia-arms-deal-in-20-years-kuala-lumpur-to-receive-new-attack-helicopters/*, accessed February 7, 2016; and Keck.

312. Lamonthe; Walton; Erik Estrada, "Philippines, U.S. begin Balikatan 2016 with Opening Ceremony," Official U.S. Marine Corps Website, April 4, 2016; USARPAC, *Partnering in the Pacific*, p. 23; Campbell and Andrews, p. 4; and Deni, *The Future of American Landpower*, p. 19.

313. USARPAC, *Partnering in the Pacific*, pp. 6-7; and Preston, p. 9.

314. De Swielande, pp. 80-81; and DoD, *U.S. Asia-Pacific Maritime Security Strategy*, p. 24.

315. Mahnken *et al.*, p. 19; Office of the Secretary of Defense, pp. 16-17; Agence France-Presse, "President Says Philippines to Spend \$1.8B on Military Modernization," DefenseNews.com, December 21, 2015, available from *www.defensenews.com/story/defense/2015/12/21/president-says-philippines-spend-military-modernization/77726792/*, accessed February 17, 2016; and Green *et al.*, p. 76.

316. Associated Press, "US Donates Vehicles to Boost Poorly-armed Philippine Forces," Military.com, December 10, 2015,

available from *www.military.com/daily-news/2015/12/10/us-donates-vehicles-boost-poorly-armed-philippine-forces.html*, accessed February 17, 2016; Moss; Baldor.

317. Green *et al.*, p. 78.

318. Walton; Green *et al.*, pp. 73-74; and Bickford *et al.*, pp. 39-40.

319. Bickford *et al.*, pp. 42-43.

320. "Hawaii National Guard Adjutant General Welcomes PHL Officials," Honolulu, HI: Philippine Consulate General, June 24, 2015, available from *www.philippineshonolulu.org/news/4597/573/HAWAII-NATIONAL-GUARD-ADJUTANT-GENERAL-WELCOMES-PHL-OFFICIALS/d,phildet/*, accessed May 17, 2017.

321. Stewart, "Marine Corps Works to Build New Ties in Southeast Asia"; and Moss.

322. Estrada; and Renato Cruz de Castro, "Balikatan Exercise Highlights Territorial Defense and Multilateral Approach," Asia Maritime Transparency Initiative, April 20, 2016, available from *amti.csis.org/balikatan-exercise-highlights-territorial-defense-multilateral-approach/*, accessed May 17, 2016.

323. Prashanth Parameswaran, "US, Philippines to Hold Amphibious Landing Exercise: PHIBLEX 2016 will be held from September 21 to October 9," Asia Defense, blog of *The Diplomat*, September 19, 2015, available from *thediplomat.com/2015/09/us-philippines-to-hold-amphibious-landing-exercise/*, accessed May 16, 2016; and "Philippine Bilateral Exercises, or 'Phiblex'," GlobalSecurity.org, last modified September 29, 2014, available from *www.globalsecurity.org/military/ops/phiblex.htm*, accessed May 16, 2016.

324. Office of the Press Secretary; and Newsham.

325. Lamonthe; Green *et al.*, p. 28; and Agence France-Presse, "Official."

326. Moss; Robson; and Lamonthe.

327. Green *et al.*, p. 77; Robson; Poling.

328. Copp; and Baldor.

329. Deni, *The Future of American Landpower*, p. 42; and Richard Javad Heydarian, "What Will a Duterte Administration Mean?" Asia Maritime Transparency Initiative, May 13, 2016, available from *amti.csis.org/will-duterte-administration-mean/*, accessed May 27, 2016.

330. Green *et al.*, pp. 32-33, 77; and Deni, *The Future of American Landpower*, p. 42.

331. Roy D. Kamphausen and Jessica Drun, "What Are Mil-Mil Ties Between the U.S. and China Good For?" War on the Rocks, April 22, 2016, available from *warontherocks.com/2016/04/what-are-mil-mil-ties-between-the-u-s-and-china-good-for/*, accessed May 22, 2016.

332. Braun, written comments to the present author, July 15, 2016.

333. Lumbers, p. 312.

334. Deni, "Strategic Landpower in the Indo-Asia-Pacific," p. 83; Fong, p. 10; Parmeter, pp. 7-8; DoD, *U.S. Asia-Pacific Maritime Security Strategy*, pp. 29-30; and Kamphausen and Drun.

335. Lowsen.

336. Kamphausen and Drun.

337. Bickford *et al.*, p. 22; and Freedberg, Jr., "Reshape US Army, Asian Alliances to Deter China."

338. USARPAC, *Partnering in the Pacific*, p. 9.

339. *Ibid.*, p. 5.

340. Stokes, pp. 12-13; and Fong, p. 12.

341. Pavgi; and Kamphausen and Drun.

342. Prashanth Parameswaran, "Underestimating US in Asia a 'Severe Miscalculation': Senior Defense Official," *Rebalance* (renamed *Trans-Pacific View*) , blog of *The Diplomat*, December 11, 2015, available from *thediplomat.com/2015/12/underestimating-us-in-asia-a-severe-miscalculation-senior-defense-official/*, accessed April 20, 2017; and Pavgi.

343. Green *et al.*, p. 173.

344. Pavgi; Freedberg, Jr., "Reshape US Army, Asian Alliances to Deter China"; and Michael A. Marra, Professor of Building Partner Capacity (BPC) Studies, School of Strategic Landpower (SSL), U.S. Army War College, Carlisle Barracks, PA, June 6, 2016, e-mail discussion with the present author.

345. DoD, *U.S. Asia-Pacific Maritime Security Strategy*, p. 29.

346. Deni, "Strategic Landpower in the Indo-Asia-Pacific," pp. 84-85; and Kamphausen and Drun.

347. Pavgi.

348. Peter Cook, "Readout of Secretary of Defense Ash Carter's Meeting With People's Republic of China's Minister of National Defense, General Chang Wanquan in Kuala Lumpur, Malaysia," Release No: NR-424-15, Washington, DC: Press Operations, U.S. Department of Defense, November 3, 2015, available from *www.defense.gov/News/News-Releases/News-Release-View/Article/627162/readout-of-secretary-of-defense-ash-carters-meeting-with-peoples-republic-of-ch*, accessed May 24, 2016; and "Senior Chinese PLA Officer Embarks on Week-Long Official Visit of the United States," The U.S.-China Policy Foundation, May 16, 2011, available from *uscpf.org/v3/2011/05/17/senior-chinese-pla-officer-visits-united-states*, accessed May 24, 2016.

349. Agence France-Presse, "Top Chinese officer pays visit to US: Pentagon," Yahoo News, June 8, 2015, available from *https://www.yahoo.com/news/top-chinese-officer-pays-visit-us-pentagon-202415362.html?ref=gs*, accessed May 24, 2016; and Li Bao, "US, China to Establish Military Dialogue," VOA News, June 13, 2015, 9:13 AM, available from *www.voanews.com/content/united-states-china-sign-deal-on-military-dialogue/2820468.html*, accessed May 24, 2016.

350. Pavgi; and "USAWC Military Engagement with PLA Academy of Military Science Back-Brief," presentation slides, U.S. Army War College, Carlisle Barracks, PA, December 16, 2015.

351. Fong, pp. 30-31.

352. Marra, e-mail, June 6, 2016.

353. Pavgi.

354. *Ibid.*

355. Office of the Secretary of Defense, p. 17.

356. Lowsen; and Bickford *et al.*, p. 36.

357. Tan, "Army seeks partnerships, new technology in the Pacific."

358. Bickford *et al.*, pp. 22, 71; and Freedberg, Jr., "Reshape US Army, Asian Alliances to Deter China."

359. Tan, "Army seeks partnerships, new technology in the Pacific."

360. Nicole Yeo, "China's Participation in Cobra Gold 2014: A Golden Opportunity for the United States?" China-US Focus, March 11, 2014, available from *www.chinausfocus.com/foreign-pol-icy/chinas-participation-in-cobra-gold-2014-a-golden-opportunity-for-the-united-states/*, accessed May 25, 2016; and Deni, "Strategic Landpower in the Indo-Asia-Pacific," pp. 84-85.

361. Henry C. O'Brien, *Peacetime Engagement of the Chinese People's Liberation Army Ground Forces by the United States Army*, Strategy Research Project, Carlisle Barracks, PA: U.S. Army War College, April 26, 2000, pp. 5-6, available from *oai.dtic.mil/oai/oai?verb=getRecord&metadataPrefix=html&identifier=ADA380135*, accessed February 19, 2016.

362. Field and Pikner.

363. O'Brien, pp. 7-8.

364. Lumbers, p. 315; and Ankit Panda, "Top US Command-er: US Won't Pursue New Bases in Australia," *Asia Defense*, blog of *The Diplomat*, August 9, 2015, available from *http://the diplomat.com/2015/08/top-us-commander-us-wont-pursue-new-bases-in-australia/*, accessed on April 28, 2017.

365. Deni, *The Future of American Landpower*, pp. x, 15.

366. Freedberg, Jr., "Reshape US Army, Asian Alliances to Deter China"; Stokes, p. 10; and Kamphausen and Drun.

367. Pavgi.

368. Although the word "danger" is part of the Chinese word for crisis (*weiji*), the other half is better translated as a more neutral "incipient moment." Benjamin Zimmer, "Crisis = Danger + Op-portunity: The Plot Thickens," *Language Log*, March 27, 2007, avail-able from *itre.cis.upenn.edu/myl/languagelog/archives/004343.html*, accessed January 21, 2016.

369. Parmeter, pp. 15-16.

370. Stokes, p. 19.

371. Teichert.

372. Braun and Lai, pp. xiii-xiv, 68-69.

373. Rapp-Hooper; and Walton.

374. J. Thomas.

375. Braun and Lai, pp. xiv-xv, 87-89.

376. David Lai, *Learning from the Stones: A Go Approach to Mas-tering China's Strategic Concept, Shi,* Carlisle, PA: Strategic Studies Institute, U.S. Army War College, 2004, p. v, available from *ssi. armywarcollege.edu/pubs/display.cfm?pubID=378,* accessed January 24, 2017.

377. Donald Trump, "President Trump's Inaugural Address, Annotated," National Public Radio, January 20, 2017, available

from *www.npr.org/2017/01/20/510629447/watch-live-president-trumps-inauguration-ceremony*, accessed January 24, 2017.

378. Midgley; and Preston, p. 11.

379. Parmeter, pp. 11-12.

380. Green *et al.*, p. 97.

381. Pavgi.

382. Braun and Lai, pp. 47-48, 103-104.

383. Stewart, "Marine Corps Works to Build New Ties in Southeast Asia"; and Newsham.

384. Michael Green, Kathleen Hicks, Mark Cancian, dirs., Zach Cooper and John Schaus, leads., *Asia-Pacific Rebalance 2025: Capabilities, Presence, and Partnerships: An Independent Review of U.S. Defense Strategy in the Asia-Pacific*, Washington, DC: Center for Strategic and International Studies, January 2016, pp. 18, 205.

385. Parameswaran, "US, Brunei Mull New Military Partnership."

386. Braun and Lai, study deliberations.

387. Bickford *et al.*, p. vii.

388. Braun and Lai, p. 53.

389. Cone, p. 10; and Cleveland, Pick, and Farris.

390. Green *et al.*, pp. 18, 132-133; and Luján, p. 5.

391. Preston, p. 17.

392. Parmeter, pp. 17-18; and Katrosh, p. 27.

393. Bickford *et al.*; and Jim Tice, "NCO, officer broadening seminars available for this summer," *Army Times*, February 23, 2015, available from *https://www.armytimes.com/story/military/*

careers/army/2015/02/23/strategic-broadening-seminars/23548367/, accessed February 2, 2017.

394. Metz; and Cleveland and Farris, p. 23.

395. Braun and Lai, pp. 69-70; and Green *et al.*, p. 113.

396. Freedberg, Jr., "SASC Pushes Bigger Army Role in Pacific Vs. China"; and Braun and Lai, pp. 70-71.

397. Braun and Lai, pp. 70-73.

398. Barno, Bensahel, and Sharp, p. 174.

399. Deni, *The Future of American Landpower*, pp. 3-4.

400. USDN, Foreword and pp. 5-2-5-3.

401. Braun and Lai, p. 45.

U.S. ARMY WAR COLLEGE

Major General William E. Rapp
Commandant

*****

STRATEGIC STUDIES INSTITUTE
and
U.S. ARMY WAR COLLEGE PRESS

Director
Professor Douglas C. Lovelace, Jr.

Director of Research
Dr. Steven K. Metz

Author
Lieutenant Colonel Clarence J. Bouchat,
U.S. Air Force (Retired)

Editor for Production
Dr. James G. Pierce

Publications Assistant
Ms. Denise J. Kersting

*****

Composition
Mrs. Jennifer E. Nevil